Plimoth Plantation

Plimoth Plantation

Then and Now

by Jean Poindexter Colby

Photographs by Plimoth Plantation, the Plymouth
Area Chamber of Commerce, and Corinthia Morss

HASTINGS HOUSE, Publishers   New York

To My Granddaughter, *Susanna Fletcher Shoham*

Second Printing, February 1972
Third Printing, February 1974

Published simultaneously in Canada by
Saunders, of Toronto, Ltd., Don Mills, Ontario

ISBN: 8038-5757-8

Library of Congress Catalog Card Number: 70-130046

Printed in the United States of America

Contents

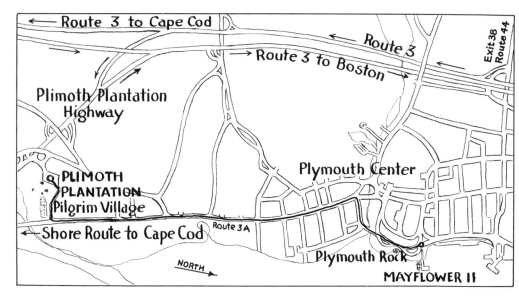

Map of Plymouth Area
—*G. F. Mason*

Acknowledgments

I wish to acknowledge the help of the entire staff of Plimoth Plantation in reading and commenting on the information in this book.

I also wish to thank my son, Peter Fletcher Colby, and Mary Rhoads, for their valued time and enthusiasm.

Author's Note

The purpose of this book is to tell the history of Plimoth Plantation in Plymouth, Massachusetts, both old and new.

The opening chapters provide background knowledge for visitors and readers who would like to supplement their vague childhood impressions with a better understanding of the Pilgrims. They give a simple view of world events during the Pilgrim era that in so many ways influenced and motivated this group. Their move to Holland, their trip on the *Mayflower* and the first seven years of their life in the New World are then briefly described. This period (1620-1627) is covered by the present Village, but the museum is now extending its presentation through 1691, when the Plantation was absorbed by the Massachusetts Bay Colony. Hence the main developments in this later period are also included here.

The book is not intended as an erudite treatise on the Pilgrims. Many fine scholars have followed their every step and have scrutinized every document left by them or written about them and their era. These in-depth studies have and will continue to add, when distilled, to our knowledge of the Pilgrims but, in some instances, have raised conflicting opinions and attitudes which are not the concern of this book. It is intended for the general reader to whom it hopes to introduce or re-introduce these people, their aims and their actions in an understandable way. It also would like to lead him on to further knowledge of them in more detailed books, and perhaps to inspire a visit to the Plantation itself.

A Guide to Original Sources Concerning Plimoth Plantation

The sources of information on the Pilgrims are multiple, varied and conflicting. Some of the early ones are straightforward eye-witness accounts while others were obviously written to promote the colonization of New England. In some cases, there are two or more versions of the same incident, while in others there is a bias because of the personal feelings of the authors toward the subject. This is especially true in the 19th and early 20th century interpretations of the Pilgrim story, with the result that the image of this group of people has become sadly distorted. Children have been given an impression that the Pilgrims were a colorless band of men, women and children who never did anything wrong, had no animal spirits, and condemned any frivolity or human enjoyment. The original sources show that not to be true at all, and it is hoped that this book will lead readers to explore further into the lives and thoughts of these people. A bibliography may be found at the back and a brief description is given here of some of the outstanding literature both by and about the Pilgrims.

*   *

Captain John Smith and his *Description of New England,* published in London in 1616, guided the Pilgrims to Cape Cod and was a source of information and possibly enthusiasm for the trip.

Other background materials include Champlain's *Les Voyages du Sieur de Champlain,* published in Paris in 1613.

There are also early letters to be found in various other volumes. Seven of these have been collected and published by the Plantation itself. *Three Visitors to Early Plymouth* (Plymouth, 1963) contains eye-witness accounts from John Pory (1572-1635),* Emmanuel Altham (1600-1635), and Isaack De Rasieres (1595-1669), all of whom actually visited the colony and wrote down their impressions.

* Birth and death dates in many cases are approximate. Careful records were not kept until much later.

In y name of god Amen· we whose names are underwriten,
the loyall subiects of our dread soueraigne Lord King Iames
by y grace of god, of great Britaine, franc, & Ireland king
defendor of y faith, &c

Haueing undertaken, for y glorie of god, and aduancemente
of y christian faith, and honour of our king & countrie, a voyage to
plant y first colonie in y Northerne parts of Virginia. doe
by these presents solemnly & mutualy in y presence of god, and
one of another, couenant, & combine our selues togeather into a
ciuill body politick; for our better ordering, & preseruation & fur=
therance of y ends aforesaid; and by vertue hearof to enacte,
constitute, and frame such just & equall Lawes, ordinance
Acts, constitutions, & offices, from time to time, as shall be thought
most meete & conuenient for y generall good of y Colonie: unto
which we promise all due submission and obedience. In witnes
wherof we haue here under subscribed our names at Cap=
Codd y ·11· of Nouember, in y year of y raigne of our soueraig
Lord king Iames of England, franc, & Ireland y eighteen
and of scotland y fiftie fourth. An: Dom·1620·]

A manuscript page from William Bradford's history, *Of Plimoth Plantation. (The Mayflower Compact)—Plimoth Plantation*

Rich material has also been found in Plymouth town and church
records.

The most important original source is William Bradford's *Of
Plimoth Plantation,** written by the many-time governor of the colony.
He started it in 1630 and finished it about 1647. The manuscript was lost
for a long time, but turned up in London after a miraculous journey and
was finally published in 1853. The recommended edition for all research-
ers is that by Worthington Chauncey Ford, originally published in two
volumes by the Massachusetts Historical Society (Boston, Houghton,
1912), now available from Atheneum Publishers in New York. A paperback edition, edited by Harvey Wish, is published by Capricorn Books in
New York.

Samuel Eliot Morison's edition of the Bradford history in one volume (New York, Knopf, 1952) is excellent for the general reader and
easier to digest. His version for young people, *The Story of the "Old
Colony" of New Plymouth* (Knopf, 1956) is also very good.

* The spelling of the name of the new plantation is taken from this book. Samuel
Eliot Morison modernized the spelling of the name in his edition.

10

Portrait of Edward Winslow by an unknown artist. Massachusetts Historical Society—*George M. Cushing*

Mourt's *Relation or Journall of the Beginnings and Proceedings of the English Plantation Settled at Plimoth in New England*—commonly known as Mourt's *Relation*—is a short and very readable account of the start of the colony. Many scholars believe it was written by Bradford and Winslow, and that Mourt or Mort was just the printer. Available in paperback edited by Dwight B. Heath (New York, Corinth Books), it is a valuable, colorful source.

Edward Winslow also wrote *Good Newes from New England* (London, 1624; reprinted by Ward 1897), an account of later events in the colony.

Nathaniel Morton wrote *New England's Memoriall* (Cambridge, 1669), which contains information on the colony's history from 1647 to 1669.

Thomas Morton, the supposed scalawag of the gay doings on Mare Mount, wrote with humor and gusto in his *New England Canaan* (Boston, Prince Society, 1883).

The famous Cotton Mather composed rather flattering biographies of the prominent Pilgrims in his *Magnalia Christi Americana,* published in London in 1702, reprinted in 1967. (New York, Russell & Russell)

Contemporary Writing on Plimoth Plantation

As has been said, much has been written about the Pilgrims, most of it unctuous in tone. However, there are several books published since World War II that present the Pilgrim story simply, clearly and without distortion.

Demos, John. *A Little Commonwealth* (New York, Oxford University Press, 1970) Family life in Plymouth Colony.

Fleming, Thomas J., *One Small Candle* (New York, Norton, 1964)

Langdon, George D., *Pilgrim Colony, A History of New Plymouth 1620–1691* (New Haven, Yale Univ. Press, 1966) Also available in paperback, published by the same press.

Leach, Douglas E., *Flintlock and Tomahawk* (New York, Macmillan, 1958) An excellent account of King Philip's War.

Rutman, Darrett B., *Husbandmen of Plymouth* (Boston, Beacon Press, 1967) A brief description of the way of life on the Plantation.

Willison, George F. *Saints and Strangers* (New York, Reynal & Hitchcock, 1945) By far the most interesting and flavorsome history of the Pilgrims from their Scrooby beginning through the expiration of the Old Colony as a separate entity. It has a valuable index, extensive notes and an annotated bibliography. Also available in paperback.

1

The World of the Pilgrims Before They Were Pilgrims

THE PILGRIMS * were the products of their times as all of us are. Because they were one of the first groups of English colonists in the New World, they have become a symbol of our earliest search for freedom and are usually associated with America and the development of the United States. On the contrary, they were closer in spirit to the mediaeval era than the later colonial one. While they helped to start a new society, they were very much part of an extremely old one.

To understand this, it is necessary to look at England and Europe in the century before the Pilgrims sailed in September, 1620, from Plymouth, England.

Rome and the Catholic Church had persisted after waves of barbarism engulfed and eventually destroyed the Roman Empire. From the 7th century A.D. to approximately 1500 the Catholic Church had gradually entrenched itself in Europe as the only Christian church, so that by 1519, when Charles V was made Holy Roman Emperor, he was also king of Spain, Sicily, Naples and Sardinia as well as lord of the Netherlands, Burgundy and the Austrian Archduchies. At that time the kingdoms of western

---

* This term, although not common until mid-19th century, will be used throughout this book for the sake of convenience.

Europe were not *nations* as we understand the word. They had shifting boundaries and many civil wars. A man's loyalty was to a person or a region, not a state.

For centuries previous to this, nobles had ruled over a feudal society in which there were mutual obligations. The word *feudal* comes from the Latin *feudum* meaning a group of estates held in return for military service to the owner of the land. By this system the nobles controlled the lands and the peasants on them, promising protection while the serfs paid homage to them and also part of what was raised.

This system was brought from France to England in the Norman Conquest (1066) and remained the way of life until commerce gradually broke up the feudal villages. Traders grouped together in towns and cities and paid enough of their newfound wealth in taxes so that the rulers were able to hire troops instead of using their own farmers. Many nobles were killed in the Crusades, which further weakened the system, and a large class of yeomen, who cultivated their own holdings and hence were called freeholders, grew up in England. "They stood below the knight and esquire because of lack of wealth rather than inferiority of birth or blood or legal privilege." * It is from this class that the Pilgrims originated as well as other groups who were becoming more and more involved in the Reformation.

This movement, while it was primarily concerned with religious reform, was also a social and political one. During the Middle Ages, the church meant everything to the common people. In the feudal villages, it was a refuge from the violence of those times just as the temples of Greece and Rome had been "by right of sanctuary." However, the Catholic church became increasingly wealthy and many churchmen abused their powers and cared little for the spiritual welfare of their people. The kings and nobles had bled the peasants to pay for their wars with the result that bitter poverty and discontent grew to unmanageable proportions.

A great wave of protest swept across Europe and England.

* Campbell, Mildred, *The English Yeoman in the Tudor and Early Stuart Age,* p. 11.

Martin Luther, the German cleric (1483–1546) really brought this "reformation" into the open when he had the effrontery to post his famous 95 theses * on the door of the church at Wittenberg. John Calvin in France (1509–1564) Huldreich Zwingli (1484–1531) in Switzerland and John Knox (1505–1572) in Scotland were other leaders who took an important part in the Reformation and the establishment of Protestant churches in northern Europe and in England and Scotland. There were massacres of Protestants in France, Germany and Spain as church and state joined in an attempt to put down the insurrections. (There were also massacres of Catholics by Protestants in some districts.) This turmoil was widespread except in the Netherlands, a country that declared itself independent of Spain in 1581, and was the first to include the mention of religious toleration in its national policy. Thus the conditions arose that influenced the Pilgrims' later move to Amsterdam.

In England, the Reformation concerned itself with the constitution of the church rather than any great change in faith. Henry VIII broke with Rome over his determination to divorce his first wife and marry again. In 1534 he announced that he was the head of the English church, and not responsible to the Pope. After which, the Archbishop of Canterbury, Thomas Cranmer, was allowed to proceed with adaptations that made the new church not very different from the old. Certainly there were the same gorgeous trappings in the ceremonies.

Protestantism received a setback in the reign of Mary, who was an ardent Catholic. She imprisoned and burned many Protestant leaders, including Cranmer. When Elizabeth I came to the throne, she again separated the Church of England from Rome, but, like her father, she did not favor any great change and gradually struck a compromise between the two factions. Hence, when it was obvious that Elizabeth would not modify the dress of the

---

* These were mostly against the Catholic system of granting indulgences to their parishioners. An indulgence was forgiveness of sin and hence a guarantee of landing in heaven after death. Such could be obtained by prayers, church attendance, or even money paid to the church. A man's credit for such good deeds was built up over the years and his chances of escaping purgatory were thus increased.

clergy and insisted on her right to control the Church of England, the objections from certain Protestant groups grew louder and louder.

These groups were called Puritans because they wanted to purify the church but it was a disparaging term, too, since they were rather high and mighty about it. They asked for reforms in liturgy and also greater strictness in religious discipline.

Some were known as Separatists since their goal was to separate from the Anglican church and form their own congregations, each of which they considered a church in itself. (The Pilgrims were in this category.) But Elizabeth would not accept any changes in the Church of England discipline or allow any group to leave it. Hence, small bands of dissenters began moving to Holland where the more liberal Dutch policy allowed them to worship as they wished.

A young man who went to Holland on a brief trip was William Brewster. He eventually became an elder, or officer, in the Pilgrim church, but at this time he was secretary to William Davison, an important emissary of Queen Elizabeth. Brewster, who had attended Cambridge University, was probably the only one of the Pilgrims with any university education. He served Davison until the latter was imprisoned on questionable charges when he went back to England. After that, Brewster eventually returned to his home in the village of Scrooby where he succeeded his

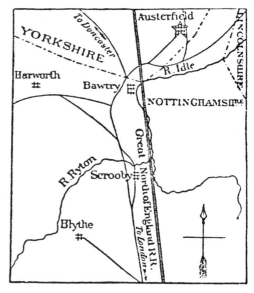

Scrooby and Austerfield— *Narrative and Critical History of America*

father as royal postmaster. This position included residence in the manor house there, which later became a meeting place of the Pilgrims.

Before starting on the actual story of the Pilgrims, it is important to take another and different kind of look at world affairs at that time—a look at cultural and scientific progress.

The Renaissance had brought about a gradual change in thinking in general and education in particular. During the Middle Ages, most education was confined to ancient universities where monks and a few nobles studied religious tracts and saw the world only in its relation to God and His outward manifestations. The Renaissance aroused interest in man and his character as well as God, and humanism became widespread. There was a gradual rediscovery of the Greek and Roman classics, which made a great impact on the writing of that period. In England, John Donne (1571–1631) composed sermons and verse about the great spiritual problems of man; Ben Jonson (1571–1637), in his court masques and plays, showed daring in depicting human love and need for beauty. William Shakespeare (1564–1616) delighted the Londoners with his varied portrayal of human character. And there were many other writers, encouraged by the new interest in man and brought to a larger audience by the invention of printing from movable type.

How much this intellectual uprising penetrated to the yeomanry of England is hard to say. Mildred Campbell in her excellent book, *The English Yeoman in the Tudor and Early Stuart Age* states that only 60–70 percent of the men could write their own names. (Women rarely received any education, and then only by tutors.) She says, "It was no disgrace in the eyes of one's fellows not to be able to read or write." * Apparently if such attainments were called for in everyday affairs, the church clerk or the town schoolmaster would help with the task. Farm lads were satisfied to pick up a little reading and writing in the local "dame schools," usually taught by women who had learned

* P. 263

17

Captain John Smith's map of New England, 1614

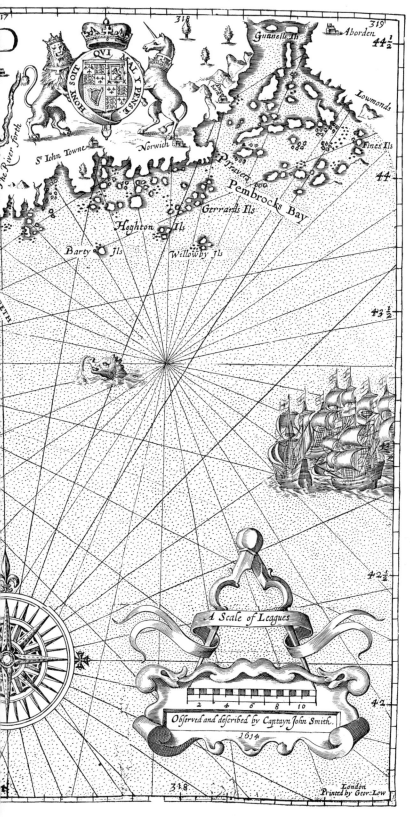

44½

HONI SOIT QVI MAL Y PENSE

Aborden

Gunnells Ils

The River Forth

St Iohn Towne   *Norwich*

Lowmonds

Fines Ils

44

P Travers poo

Pembrocks Bay

Gerrards Ils

Hoghton   Ils

43½

Barty   Ils   *Willowby Ils*

43

42½

A Scale of Leagues

2	4	6	8	10

42

Observed and described by Captayn John Smith.

1614

London
Printed by Geor: Low

these arts in some way and wanted to add to their scanty livelihood. There was no law that said anyone had to go to school at all.

How many of the Pilgrims could read or write is unknown. Obviously most of the leaders could. Some of them like Robinson, Brewster and Bradford wrote very well indeed. Books are mentioned as part of their household goods and news of the New World explorations had obviously reached them even before they left for Holland. Actually, English transatlantic voyages had started over a century before that. John Cabot crossed the ocean in 1497 and 1498, and his son, Sebastian, in 1505. Francis Drake returned from circumnavigating the world in 1580 in the ship, the *Golden Hind,* and some of the Pilgrims might very well have heard about his triumphant welcome home to London, similar to a present-day astronaut's. Martin Pring, Captain Gosnold, Martin Frobisher, Humphrey Gilbert and Walter Raleigh all pressed on to the New World for English companies or with private funds. France sent Jean Maillard in 1542, Champlain in 1603 and 1605, while the Dutch followed suit with Henry Hudson in 1609 and Adrian Block in 1614. And, of course, Captain John Smith's explorations were widely known. It was his map, published in 1614, that the Pilgrims may have consulted before their voyage.

After that the traffic across the ocean was not exactly crowded but there were too many recorded expeditions to mention here. Some were for trading, others for exploration and colonization.

Hence it is clear that the Pilgrims' trip in 1620 was not epoch-making as a voyage except that they sailed alone. They made it in a chartered ship, just as a group might charter an airplane now. Other passengers, not of their religious beliefs, joined them. In short, the voyage of the *Mayflower* was not remarkable for those times but the result was.

2

The Pilgrims as a Separatist Group

Life In England and Holland

WHEN Queen Elizabeth died in 1603 and James VI of Scotland was named James I of England, hope ran high that he might be more liberal toward the Puritans. James, however, was too pleased with his sudden wealth and power to encourage new movements in religion. Furthermore, he wanted no challenge to his authority. The Presbyters or elders in the Scottish church had always been a thorn in his royal side, so when a delegation of bishops and other churchmen, including four Puritans, presented a list of requests for church reform at Hampton Court, he would grant only a few. In fact, at the first meeting of Parliament he vowed to harry any nonconformists out of the land, and to show he meant business, he imprisoned the Puritans who had presented the petition.

One good thing did come out of this Hampton Court meeting. James accepted a proposal by one of the Puritans that the Bible then used differed too much from the original Hebrew and should be rewritten. He ordered the most learned of scholars at Oxford and Cambridge Universities to work on translating a new Bible. This resulted in the King James Version, still in use today and considered one of the most beautiful pieces of prose in the English language. It was not the one, however, that the Pilgrims used. Theirs was the Geneva Bible.*

To return to Scrooby, a small village in Nottinghamshire, we find William Brewster established as royal postmaster and living in the manor house. In a few years he must have heard of a small group of dissenters who were holding separate religious meetings because of their objections to the Anglican Church. He soon joined them in spite of the edict by King James against such groups. In fact, as has been said, their secret meetings were often held at the manor, probably one reason they were discovered by the royal officials.

A newcomer to the group was a young man named William Bradford. An orphan, he lived with his uncles, Thomas and Robert Bradford, whose farm was just two miles from Scrooby in the small village of Austerfield. They opposed William's attendance at these Separatist meetings, but he continued to worship with this band and his youthful enthusiasm must have meant much to them. At this time he was probably around 17 or 18 years old—a surmise because only the date of his christening is known. However, in those days christenings usually followed shortly after birth because of the high death rate in children.

Actually, the Pilgrims were *all* young at this time, even though they are often thought of as old and staid. With the exception of Brewster and Carver, it is estimated that they were in their mid-twenties when the move to Holland was suggested.

Brewster was summoned before the Commissioners of the Prince of York because of his part in the Pilgrim meetings and the postmastership was taken from him. However, the meetings were continued secretly elsewhere with Richard Clifton as minister, and plans were made to leave for Holland as soon as practical matters were settled.

And what "matters" these must have been. How heart-

---

* The Geneva Bible was first published in 1560 just after Elizabeth came to the throne. Geneva had become a haven for many fugitives from religious persecution and included some of the great minds of the century, such as John Calvin. A facsimile edition of the Bible was brought out by the University of Wisconsin Press in 1969.

wrenching were the decisions to leave their neat farms and rich fields; their relatives, neighbors and friends. For, as far as can be ascertained, these people were sturdy farmers whose families had lived on their land for generations. Their station in life was a respectable, independent one.

Furthermore, the move to Holland was away from their peaceful country life to that of a bustling city where they would know no trades and would have to struggle with a foreign language.

All of these problems and many dire possibilities must have weighed upon them. Yet they went forward with their plans, selling their lands and other possessions, and chartered a Dutch ship to take them to Amsterdam. Then, once stowed on board, their passage paid, they were betrayed by their captain to the local authorities. At that time it was unlawful for any English person to leave the country without permission, so they were all imprisoned.

It was not for long, but when they were liberated the question was again—what to do? Now they had no homes left and no one to help them find food or lodging. They had literally burned their bridges.

Still, there is no better example of the old adage, "Where there's a will there's a way," than the Pilgrims. A few faint-hearted souls gave up but most of the group sold enough of the possessions and stores they had planned on taking to Amsterdam to charter another Dutch boat.

They had to steal away to it in the greatest secrecy as their every move was now watched, but the ship did appear at the appointed time and place and a boatload of men got safely on it. The women and children, though, were on another craft and were stranded on a sandbar at low tide. The captain was going to wait for the tide to rise but he thought he saw official-looking men galloping toward the shore. Whereupon he hurriedly decided to sail away while he could with those passengers already on board.

Much moaning and wailing came from both parties as husbands and wives, fathers and children were separated. On the boat that set off for Amsterdam the cries of distress soon changed to the groans of seasickness as a monstrous storm was encountered and the little ship was driven away off course along the coast of Norway.

Both crew and passengers thought their hour had come as huge waves beat over the craft with winds near hurricane force. That it eventually blew itself out without loss of life seemed an act of God to the English group and even to the crew, so bad had been the storm. They eventually did reach Amsterdam and, after some weeks and months, were rejoined by their loved ones whom they had left stranded. The latter made their way to Holland in twos and threes and great must have been their rejoicing when they all arrived.

The first months in Amsterdam were naturally ones of confusion. They found there two earlier English Separatist groups as well as many Protestants who had come from Antwerp and other towns in what is now called Belgium. Spain still ruled there with an iron hand, driving out these Huguenots, many of whom were skilled craftsmen.

Since the Pilgrims were unskilled they had to take menial jobs and live in cramped quarters. William Bradford, for instance, became an apprentice to a Huguenot silk weaver. Before long poverty was upon them and the future looked dark.

However, the problems and the difficulty of learning the language could have been surmounted if they had been able to worship in peace. Instead of the unity of thought and spiritual goals that they expected to share with the other Separatist groups that had come to Holland earlier, they found wrangling and bickering. This mounted to such proportions that after a year they decided to leave Amsterdam for Leyden while they still possessed a separate entity and clear purpose.

Leyden was a beautiful little city at the mouth of the Rhine with an old university where the atmosphere was scholarly rather than political. Eleven years the Pilgrim group spent there, and in the light of later events, one would call this period meaningful in that it prepared this little Separatist band in many ways for their American venture. They solidified as a religious and civic group and they found they could endure against great odds.

Shortly after their arrival they bought a house on Bell Street for their pastor, John Robinson, and held their meetings in one of its rooms. It had land behind it where eventually they built a group of little houses for the congregation.

William Bradford soon found a position with another weaver and, since space was crowded, he roomed in the house with William Brewster. From him and other local savants he soon learned French as well as Dutch and also picked up some Hebrew. This was important as Pilgrim theology was based on the belief that they should live according to God's Word as expressed in the Bible.

Poverty was not far from their doors even during this period, but the years in Leyden were notable for their peace and unification. Children were born who brought happiness and swelled the Pilgrim numbers, and families settled down to living and learning, worshipping as they had always wanted to do. However, even though they were working hard and were reaffirming their belief in the pure, simple worship of God, the older men like William Brewster kept their eyes on the political situation. By 1616, the twelve years' truce between Spain and the Netherlands had but four more years to go. The Pilgrim leaders worried about what would happen at its end. Probably, they thought, there would be religious persecution even worse than what they had experienced in England, and they again would have to move on. They feared the Spanish inquisition and eventual conquest of Holland by Spain. Also their children were slowly becoming more Dutch than English. They spoke Dutch fluently and had taken with alacrity to the easy-going Dutch ways. On Sunday, for instance, the Dutch would dance and make merry after their church services. They did not believe as the Pilgrims did that it should be a whole day of prayer, sermons and spiritual contemplation.

For these reasons and the fear that they might eventually

lose their identity as a group, they decided to leave Holland and take passage for the "Northern Part of Virginia" or the Hudson River region. This was near where Captain John Smith of England had led two successful expeditions. The excitement and possibilities of this newly opened land had reached the Pilgrims before they left for Holland. Captain Smith himself had aroused the populace with his *Description of New England,* as has been mentioned, and in 1605 several Indians had been brought from "Virginia" to London, where their accounts of their homeland and their strong, commanding physique had stirred great enthusiasm for further exploration and settlement. And free land was offered! It was an unheard-of opportunity.

Still, to leave for the wilderness was a big move and many who were faint-hearted or physically frail elected to stay behind. The others sent Robert Cushman and John Carver off to London to interview members of the Virginia Company for a patent or land grant.* To be sure, a Dutch Company offered to give them free passage and free land if they would settle in New Netherland, part of the Dutch claim in the New World, but the Pilgrims decided that that would mean more of the earthly temptations they objected to in Leyden. Guiana, Walter Raleigh's promised land, was another possibility. There, he said, the weather was always warm, gold was plentiful, and food and wild life existed just for the taking. But a crown or royal colony the Pilgrims wanted no part of, so "Hudson's River" was decided upon as their destination.

Unfortunately, when Carver and Cushman reached London, the terms demanded by the Virginia Company were staggeringly high. After many weeks of meetings, the negotiators, brought back to Holland a discouraging report.

Then one Thomas Weston, a London merchant and a born promoter, approached them. He was a member of a group called

* Morison says in a footnote on p. 34 of Bradford's history: ". . . these patents for 'particular plantations' never did specify where the plantation was to be located; the leaders were supposed to report at Jamestown and select a tract of land not already granted. It is not inconceivable that local authorities in Virginia would have welcomed an outpost against Dutch and French encroachments to the north."

the London Adventurers who loaned money to would-be traders and colonists. A new offer was made. John Robinson and other leaders were the negotiators this time and the discussion lasted for months, but again the terms seemed too weighted against them. They were to work only for the Adventurers, not for themselves, and were not to own the houses they built on the land they cleared until after seven years, when all capital and profit would be divided among the stockholders.

It was a hard bargain indeed but by this time the Pilgrims who had decided to go had disposed of their lands and goods in Holland. They had bought the *Speedwell* to take them to England where they planned to charter a larger ship, the *Mayflower,* for the final voyage across the Atlantic. The *Speedwell* was to accompany the *Mayflower* and was supposed to stay in the New World for their use in exploring and fishing.

Back in Holland the *Speedwell* was overhauled; new and larger masts were stepped in and all was ready for departure from Delfthaven, a coastal town 20 miles from Leyden. Then followed a very sad leave-taking. Pastor John Robinson elected to stay behind to care for the group remaining in Holland, planning to follow later after a foothold had been made on the new continent.

William Brewster and William Bradford were among the leaders of the "planters" or would-be colonists departing along with Bradford's young wife, Dorothy, a girl from the "Ancient Brethren," one of the Separatist groups they had left behind in Amsterdam. They had been married Nov. 13, 1613.

On the way to England, the *Speedwell* sailed poorly, and was caulked and repaired on arrival at Southampton where the *Mayflower* was waiting. Other passengers, strangers to the Pilgrims, joined them there, having been recruited by Thomas Weston to increase the number of able men.

One of them was John Alden, a young man of 18, who was signed on as a cooper or barrel-maker. This was one of the requisites of all vessels leaving England at that time. In the case of the Pilgrims such a man was badly needed to make the barrels necessary to hold the grain and other items the colonists were to send back to pay off their debts. Myles Standish and his wife, Rose, also joined the group. He had met the members in Holland where he was stationed as an English soldier, and had been hired to go with them. His military training was to stand the colonists in good stead.

The Voyage on the *Mayflower*

It is well known how the ships set forth from Southampton on August 5, 1620 * and how the *Speedwell* again started to leak. Both ships put into Dartmouth and waited while she was repaired and once more declared sound and ready for the ocean voyage. They sailed August 23rd but again she handled badly and leaked, so, accompanied by the *Mayflower,* she turned back and put into Plymouth harbor.

It was then decided to abandon the *Speedwell* and continue with the *Mayflower* alone. A few more Separatists gave up at the thought of the dubious accommodations—as well they might— but 102 passengers crowded aboard and sailed away on September 6, 1620.

Of this 102, only three—William Brewster, his wife, and William Bradford—came from the original Scrooby group. Forty- one (including 14 children) were of the Leyden congregation. Completing the number were the recent recruits, who came to be known as "strangers" or unknown to the Pilgrims, while the Pilgrims were called "saints."—This word was used in the Biblical sense as one of God's chosen people, not as one canonized by the Catholic Church. In addition, about 20 ** were in the crew. There were also a few mercenaries.

Some were indeed quite strange to the Pilgrims, not only in their religious beliefs but also in their manners and general con-

---

* The dates in the old accounts were figured according to the Old Style or Julian Calendar, which ran about ten days earlier than ours.
** Again the exact number is subject to question. There was no log kept of the *Mayflower* voyage and no actual passenger list but Bradford's history does name most of the passengers and some of the crew.

As the original *Mayflower* might have looked. (The *Mayflower II* under full sail)—*Plymouth Area Chamber of Commerce*

duct. However, the basic difference between the two was a religious one. The Pilgrims considered themselves to be the elect of God. They had entered into a covenant with Him and were sure of special consideration from Him, especially in life after death. The Strangers, on the other hand, were definitely not part of this select group, and were therefore not invited to worship with them. It is interesting to note, though, that several of them *did* become Pilgrim leaders—John Alden, for instance.

Because the genealogy of *Mayflower* descendants is of interest to all Americans, especially to those who claim relationship, a list follows of the *Mayflower* passengers. The wives and children of the men who married after their arrival are not included. Those who arrived later on the *Fortune,* the *Little James,* the *Anne* and other so-called Pilgrim ships, are also not included. (They may be found in the appendix of George Willison's *Saints and Strangers,* in Part II of Charles Edward Banks' *The Planters of the Commonwealth,* and other volumes.)

The names are grouped under the head of the family to whom they were related or whom they served as stewards, servants or "bound" children. In those days in London it was a common practice for waifs or orphans to be bound to a man with an obligation to serve him until they came of age (21). The More children (see William Brewster and John Carver) were examples. *Master* was a term used for men with sufficient means to have servants, but the latter were not house or body servants. Most of them were young men whose fare was paid, in return for which they were expected to do hard, manual labor for seven years of "indenture" without pay.

The letter *S* indicates passengers not in the Leyden congregation. The spellings of the names vary greatly. Ages at the time of sailing are estimated in parentheses, where possible.

S Alden, John (18) cooper
Allerton, Master Isaac (32) a tailor
   from London
   Wife, Mary (__)*
   Son, Bartholomew (8)
   Daughters, Remember (6) and
     Mary (4)
   John Hooke, servant-boy
S Billington, John (30)
   Wife, Ellen (28)
   Sons, Francis (9) and John (6)
   (These ages are in grave doubt.)
Bradford, Master William (36) a

silk weaver, later Governor
   Wife, Dorothy (23)
Brewster, Master William (__)
   printer, publisher and ruling
   Elder
   Wife, Mary (31)
   Sons, Love (9) and Wrestling
     (6)
   Two bound boys, Richard More
     and his brother, both probably under 10, of a family
     of orphaned children.
S Britteridge, Richard (__)

* (__) indicates that age is not known

S Browne, Peter (___)
Carver, Master John (54) merchant, Deacon and later Governor
  Wife, Catherine (___) Also spelled Katherine, or Katharine
  Desire Minter (16) companion
  Roger Wilder (21) and William Lathem or Latham (16) servants
  Jasper More, bound boy (see note under *Brewster*)
  John Howland, (27) steward-servant
S Chilton, James (57) tailor
  Wife, Susanna (—)
  Daughter, Mary (15)
Cooke, Francis (43) wool-comber
  Son, John (10)
Crackstone, John (___) Also spelled Crackston or Crakston
  Son, John (___)
S Eaton, Francis (25) carpenter
  Wife, Sarah (___)
S Ellis, _____ (___) sailor
S English, Thomas (___) mariner
Fletcher, Moses (___) blacksmith or shipsmith
S Fuller, Edward (25)
  Wife, Anne (___)
  Son, Samuel, infant
Fuller, Master Samuel (35) deacon and physician
  William Butten, servant-boy, died on the voyage
S Gardiner, Richard (20)
Goodman, John (25) linen weaver
S Hopkins, Master Stephen (35)
  Wife, Elizabeth (___)
  Sons, Giles (15), Oceanus (born at sea)
  Daughters, Constance (11), Demaris (3)
  Servants, Edward Dotey and Edward Leister
S Margeson, Edmund (___)
S Martin, Master Christopher (45) representative of the Merchant Adventurers
  Wife _____ (___)

Servants, Solomon Prower (___), John Langemore (___)
S Mullins, Master William (40) shopkeeper
  Wife, Alice (___)
  Daughter, Priscilla (18) married John Alden
  Son, Joseph (6)
  Servant, Robert Carter
Priest, Degory (41) hatter
S Rigdale, John (___)
  Wife, Alice (___)
Rogers, Thomas (___) cloth merchant
  Son, Joseph (12)
S Samson, Henry (___)
S Standish, Myles (34) military leader
  Wife, Rose (___)
Tilley, Edward (___) cloth maker
  Wife, Anne (___)
  Two cousins, Humility Cooper and Henry Samson, young children.
Tilley, John (___)
  Wife, Elizabeth (35)
  Daughter, Elizabeth (14) married John Howland
Tinker, Thomas (___) wood sawyer
  Wife, _____ (___)
  Son, _____ (___)
S Trevore, William (___) sailor
Turner, John (___)
  Two sons (— —)
S Warren, Master Richard (40)
White, Master William (28) wool carder
  Wife, Susanna (26)
  Son, Peregrine, born on the *Mayflower*
  Servants, Ellen More (see note under *Brewster*), a child
  George Soule (20)
S Williamson, Thomas (___)
Winslow, Edward (25) printer, holder of many offices at the Plantation
  Wife, Elizabeth (23)
S Winslow, Gilbert (20) younger brother of Edward

No actual specifications of the *Mayflower* have ever been found but it is generally agreed she was a simple trading ship chartered for a purpose. Even the name *Mayflower* was common. After she took the Pilgrims to Cape Cod, she stayed close by to offer them shelter until the following April. Then she sailed back to London, probably to take other cargoes, human and material, to other ports. Little valid information has been found except the fact she was the subject of an Admiralty survey on the Thames River in 1624.

There was no usual passenger allotment for a cargo ship this size (104' overall). However, when 102 were crowded between decks, conditions must have been very uncomfortable. Food was cooked over a smoky open fire when the weather allowed it but was mostly eaten cold because of frequent storms. There was no provision for sanitation or for washing of clothes or bodies. Master * Christopher Jones was the only one who had a cabin to himself. For the others the odor of seasickness, spoiled food, human excrement, perspiration, soiled clothes and bed linen must have been overpowering.

And yet only one of the passengers died—Dr. Samuel Fuller's servant boy—and his place was immediately filled by a new arrival. Mrs. Stephen Hopkins gave birth to a boy, appropriately called Oceanus.

Immediately after the *Mayflower* set sail alone, the wrangling began between the different factions of passengers and also the crew. Master Jones, an experienced seaman and a man whose stature as a friend and protector of the Pilgrims has increased over the years of research on this group, watched the situation with a wary eye. He knew how easily dissension among the passengers could spread to the crew. He also knew that his discipline of the seamen should be confined to the dangerous and exhausting labors on the sails and riggings required by an old ship like the *Mayflower,* especially at that stormy, perilous time of year. Hence when they taunted the Pilgrims for the frequent

---

* In those days the *master* of a ship controlled its navigation. The *captain* was in charge of military defense and business transactions.

1. Captain's Charthouse	4. Steerage	7. Fo'c'sle	10. The Tween Decks
2. Quarterdeck	5. Capstan	8. The Tiller Flat	11. Anchor Windlass
3. Great Cabin	6. Main Deck	9. Beakhead	12. Main Hold

prayer meetings and psalm singing, their oaths and obscenities went unrestrained.

One sailor in particular, the boatswain's mate, took pleasure in ridiculing the "glib-gabbety puke-stockings" as the crew called them. He cursed them daily and seemed untamable until one day after they had been out on the Atlantic about two weeks, he was suddenly taken sick. Many are the theories of what disease he and other later victims succumbed to. Certainly the food by that time had become weevily and half rotten. Scurvy, prevalent because of the restricted diet, was common. Exposure to the cold and dampness did not help, and there was always the possibility of acute appendicitis or heart failure even in one so young. Samuel Fuller, the supposed doctor of the Pilgrims, had no real medical degree and probably little actual training. However, the medical beliefs and treatment of the day could not have been more inaccurate or ineffective by modern standards. The various fluids or "humors" of the body were supposed to be vital and the favorite remedies for any illness were purging, bloodletting and the application of leeches to draw off blood from the afflicted parts. Herbs were much used—and the Pilgrims were to note with interest the pres-

33

ence of herbs, especially sassafras, when they later explored Cape Cod and the Plymouth area.*

Whatever the cause, the poor boatswain's mate sickened and died in a few days and his sudden demise was looked upon by many, especially the religious minded, as a possible act of God against a man who had reviled this group of "saints." Certainly relations between crew and passengers were eased after his unexpected death.

Master Jones must have been relieved by this as all his attention and abilities were soon engaged in keeping the *Mayflower* afloat. A tremendous Arctic storm engulfed them when they were halfway across the Atlantic. Great waves broke over the ship, sails were furled and all passengers commanded to remain between decks. A main beam gave way that caused the main deck to leak and let in sea water and rain on those below. The horrifying question came up as to whether they should not turn back, but the Pilgrims prayed and "committed themselves to the will of God to proceed," according to William Bradford. They also remembered a "great iron screw" which they had brought along from Holland to assist in holding together the houses they intended to build. With its help the split beam was secured in place and shortly after that Master Jones decided to stay on the appointed course.

Eventually the storm abated but the waves were still mountainous. Master Jones continued to keep everyone below decks where the living must have been dreadful. Fuel had given out. The passengers' supply of meat and beer was almost exhausted. The water was slimy and ill-smelling.

Finally the weather cleared. The white-faced group came out blinking into the unaccustomed sunshine. For days there still was only a vast expanse of heaving ocean to look at but early one

* At that time sassafras tea was considered the cure for almost every ill and drew a high price in London. One of the first things the Pilgrims did in Plymouth was to plant herb gardens close by their houses, as plants like sage, sassafras, rosemary, marjoram, thyme and dill were used to treat sickness and also to preserve food. Since there was no refrigeration the latter was very important. Those little gardens are very much a part of the present Plantation and add charm and authentic pungency to the cooking that is done in some of the houses.

morning, November 9th, Master Jones made out a gull in the dim light of dawn. The leadsman, whose job was to sound the depth of the water, called out that he had at last struck bottom at 80 fathoms.* Soon after, the lookout high up on the mainmast sang out the welcome words, LAND HO!

One of the literary understatements of all times appears in Mourt's *Relation* to describe this moment:

"Upon the ninth of November, after many difficulties in boisterous storms, by God's will, we sighted land to be Cape Cod [named by Bartholomew Gosnold in 1602] which afterward it proved to be. . . . The appearance of it much comforted us, especially seeing such a broad land that was wooded to the edge of the sea. It caused us to rejoice together, and praise God that had allowed us once again to see land." **

The journey that took 65 days of "long beating at sea" was over.

Probably, the slow, interminable voyage irked the passengers just as delays nowadays irritate plane and train customers. At any rate, before they reached land, several of the grumbling men mentioned that once off the ship they would do what they wanted and act as they pleased. They could not wait for their feet to touch land to be on their own.

This lack of unity disturbed the leaders of the Pilgrim group who realized that unless they held together and faced the obstacles of the wilderness with combined strength, both physical and spiritual, they would not live long. Word of the failure of various other settlements in Maine and Virginia had reached their ears before they sailed and they did not want to share a similar fate.

For that reason, after the *Mayflower* had encountered high seas and shoal water on the Monomoy (Chatham) side of the Cape and had turned back north to anchor in the hook of what is now Provincetown Harbor, an historic meeting was called and a

* A fathom is six feet.
** P. 15

35

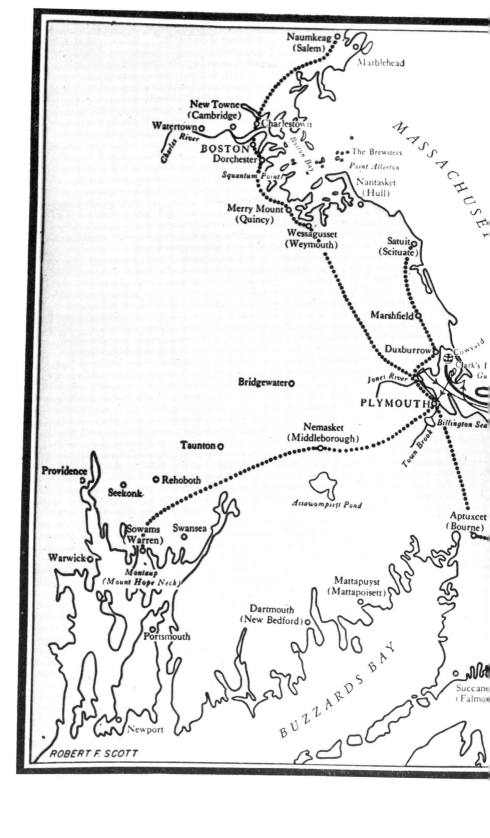

Naumkeag
(Salem)

Marblehead

MASSACHUSE

New Towne
(Cambridge)

Watertown

Charles River

Charlestown

BOSTON

Dorchester

Squantum Point

Boston Bay

The Brewsters
Point Allerton

Nantasket
(Hull)

Merry Mount
(Quincy)

Wessagusset
(Weymouth)

Satuit
(Scituate)

Marshfield

Duxburrow

Coward
Clark's I
Gu

Bridgewater

Jones River

PLYMOUTH

Billington Sea

Nemasket
(Middleborough)

Town Brook

Taunton

Providence

Rehoboth

Seekonk

Assawompsett Pond

Aptuxcet
(Bourne)

Sowams
(Warren)

Swansea

Warwick

Montaup
(Mount Hope Neck)

Mattapuyst
(Mattapoisett)

Dartmouth
(New Bedford)

Portsmouth

BUZZARDS BAY

Succane
(Falmo

Newport

ROBERT F. SCOTT

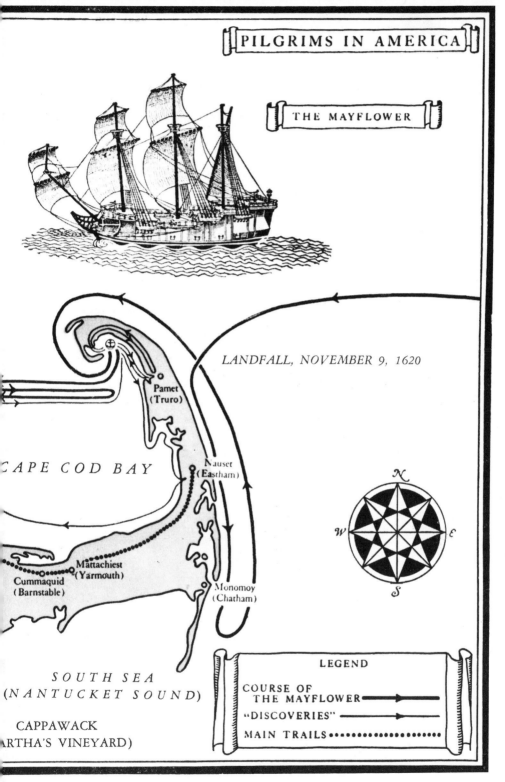

The course of the *Mayflower*, the "Discoveries," and the main Indian trails at the time—*Plimoth Plantation*

very important document was drawn up: *The Mayflower Compact*.* (This may be seen in script on page 10) It was signed by 41 of the 51 men on board. Of these only 6 were from the Leyden group: William Bradford, William Brewster, Samuel Fuller, Isaac Allerton, Francis Cooke and Edward Winslow.

The original of the *Compact* was never found but the text was published in Mourt's *Relation,* William Bradford's *Of Plimoth Plantation* and Nathanial Morton's *New England's Memoriall*. These three inclusions make it obvious that this agreement was considered as important then as it now seems today. Since that time historians, political scholars and writers, especially of the old school, have called it the basis of the town meeting form of government, our outright ownership of land, our political autonomy, and many other things. Here it is, somewhat modernized in language.

THE COMPACT

"In the name of God, Amen. We whose names are underwritten, the loyal subjects of our dread sovereign, Lord, King James, by the grace of God, of Great Britain, France and Ireland King, defender of the faith, etc., having undertaken, for the glory of God, and advancement of the Christian faith, and honor of our King and country, a voyage to plant the first colony in the northern parts of Virginia, do by these presents solemnly and mutually in the presence of God, and one of another, covenant and combine ourselves together into a civil body politic, for our better ordering and preservation and furtherance of the ends aforesaid; and by virtue hereof to enact, constitute and frame such just and equal laws, ordinances, acts, constitutions and offices from time to time, as shall be thought most meet and convenient for the general good of the colony, unto which we promise all due submission and obedience. In witness whereof, we have hereunder subscribed our names at Cape Cod, the 11th of November, in the year of the reign of our sovereign Lord, King James of England, France, and Ireland the eighteenth, and of Scotland the fifty fourth. Anno Domini. 1620"

Robert Moody, in the *Old South Meeting House Leaflet* #225, calls it: "A straight-forward solution of an immediate problem which confronted the founders of the Plymouth Colony —how to prevent factionalism and to promote the common welfare. . . . There was within this simple covenant the seed of self government." Samuel Eliot Morison says, "They intended this government to be only temporary until they could obtain a patent

* It was so named later.

38

The signing of the *Mayflower Compact* is portrayed on board the *May-flower II* by mannequins—*Plimoth Plantation*

from the Council of New England or a charter from the King. But it remained the basis of their government for ten years; some say for 70 years since all their later government developed out of the Compact." *

Every able man (even the trouble makers) supposedly signed it. Of the 41 who did sign, 12 were of the "master" rating. Of these, John Carver supposedly signed first, followed by William Bradford, Edward Winslow, William Brewster, Myles Standish, William Mullins, William White, Richard Warren, Stephen Hopkins and others. They were followed by 27 "goodmen" who were next in the social order. They were independent workers such as craftsmen, apprentices or sailors. Four servants also signed.

* Morison, S. E., *The Story of the "Old Colony" of New Plymouth,* p. 45

The 13 who did not sign included sons of the signers, hence already represented, along with nine servants and two sailors, who presumably were under age or ill at the time. John Carver was confirmed governor, the only official mentioned.

Life in America

The Provincetown anchorage was well protected but the ship had to stay three-quarters of a mile off shore because of shallow water. The frequent trips to the beach in the cold, rainy November weather started colds and coughs that undoubtedly led to pneumonia and undermined the strength of this exhausted, poorly fed group. The many deaths that winter can be blamed at least in part on this initial exposure.

However, the land at Cape Cod *did* look good to the Pilgrims and their fellow passengers, and a small party was immediately sent ashore in the long boat, wading the last hundred yards hip deep in the icy waves. Wood and water, both of which they needed badly, were found in abundance and carried back to the ship. Some women did washing, and probably the children ran up and down the beach.

On November 13th the shallop, a 30-foot sailing and rowing craft that they had brought with them partly assembled, was unshipped and her seams found to be opened. It took over two weeks for the carpenter to make the necessary repairs. In the meantime 16 armed men under the command of Myles Standish went ashore in the ship's long boat and sighted a group of five or six Indians and a dog. When the natives saw the *Mayflower* contingent they fled into the woods where Standish and his band followed them but never caught up. The pursuers covered quite a bit of ground in their chase, noting the land and trees, and eventually coming upon an old Indian cornfield along with burial mounds and platforms. Still further on they found the remains of a house and huge kettle, probably taken by the Indians from a shipwreck. Nearby was a sand heap that had been newly piled and into which they dug. Soon they turned up baskets of Indian corn, some of which they took back to the ship. A guard was set that evening but the night was uneventful as were their continued explorations the next day. They found more evidence of Indian occupation—in fact, William Bradford was caught in a deer snare while they were looking over the terrain. But they saw no Indians. On return to the ship, they decided to keep the corn for seed next spring and to replace or pay for it when they had the chance. (They did pay for it eventually.)

On the second expedition, both the shallop and the long boat were taken and 34 men went ashore. Their purpose was to locate a spot for permanent settlement with fresh water and a good harbor available, but they could not find one. That afternoon they shot three fat geese and six ducks which they roasted for supper. To quote from Mourt's *Relation,* "We ate with soldier's stomachs, for we had eaten little all that day." *

The next morning they discovered a canoe by a stream and then went back to the cache of corn where they uncovered ten more bushels. Some of the men took this back to the ship while a

* P. 25

A replica of the shallop approaches Long Beach off modern Plymouth
—*Plimoth Plantation*

group of the strongest continued their search for further corn supplies and Indian settlements. The following day two of the sailors came upon two abandoned wigwams and found graves in which finely made bows, dishes, bowls, and strings and bracelets of beads had been placed. The weather having turned very cold and stormy, they returned to the *Mayflower* to tell of their discoveries.

On December 6th the shallop again set out carrying ten men in charge of Myles Standish, who had become the military leader of the Pilgrims. The weather was "cold and hard" * and they began the trip by getting stuck on a sand bar. Apparently they had to wait hours for the tide to come in, during which time two men were taken ill and one almost fainted from the cold. One of the sailors, a gunner, also became very sick and remained so . . . small wonder as they all sat in an open boat, unable to move about. Finally they could hoist the sails and make good progress along the shore although a biting wind froze their clothes like "coats of iron." After sailing "six or seven leagues," equivalent to approximately 20 miles, they saw on the shore at the entrance of what is now Eastham Harbor a group of Indians working over "a big black thing." This turned out to be a blackfish or small whale. The Indians ran off when an exploring party approached. The men followed their footprints in the sand until they disappeared in the woods. Further on, up what is now Wellfleet Bay, they came upon some Indian houses, a burial ground and corn fields.

Being weary and cold, at nightfall they set up camp—a hastily built barricade—at Great Meadow Creek. About midnight their sleep was rudely interrupted by fiendish yells from the woods, and cries from their sentries to arm themselves. The yells died down and nothing happened until suddenly, just before dawn when they were preparing to embark in the shallop but could not because of low tide, more savage cries rang out and arrows began to pour at them from the woods.

The party on the shallop was cut off as it was decided some

* Mourt's *Relation,* ed. D. B. Heath, p. 41.

should defend their one means of transportation. Hence several men were on the boat; the rest stood to defend the barricade. It must have been a tense moment, for they could tell by the Indian yells that they were greatly outnumbered. Standish, however, told them not to fire their muskets until they could see their enemies. In the half light this was difficult but finally one especially daring brave could be made out behind a tree half a musket shot away. He let loose with many arrows but the Pilgrims were able to duck or dodge them. Three musket shots were fired at him, one finally hitting the tree, and all the red men fled.

It is a nice commentary on the Pilgrim courage that instead of breathing a sigh of relief and escaping in the shallop, they followed the retreating Indians, finally shooting off a couple of muskets "that they might see we were not afraid of them nor discouraged." *

After this first encounter with the Indians, who were later identified as of the warlike Nauset tribe, they boarded the shallop and sailed down the cape to "Thievish Harbor" (previously described by other explorers and named Plimoth by Captain John Smith) only to meet up with a terrible northeaster just as they entered the bay. Its ferocity frightened them and no wonder as their mast was broken and the boat almost wrecked in the breakers. So, well drenched, they took shelter on an island nearby, which they later named after one of their number, the mate on the *Mayflower*, Mr. Clarke. He was the first to step ashore according to some accounts.

The next day, December 9th, they explored the island. The following day being Sunday, they did not work. Undoubtedly the physical rest helped them but the members of the crew were more than impatient at their taking time off just when it was desperately necessary to spend every waking moment in finding a place for permanent settlement. This respect for the Sabbath is commented upon many times in the old records until it becomes obvious that the crew and all others not of the Pilgrim faith reluctantly grew to respect this determined devotion to spiritual

* Mourt's *Relation*, ed. D. B. Heath, p. 36

matters. The Pilgrims started and ended each day with prayer and when they escaped disaster—as they continually did—they fell on their knees to thank Almighty God for their deliverance.

On December 11th or what is now called "Forefathers' Day" in Plymouth, the men in the shallop navigated Plymouth Harbor and explored the coast. They liked what they saw, although they were of two minds as to whether to settle inland up Jones River (named for the master of the *Mayflower*) in the woods whose timber they badly needed, or near the coast where there was a high hill they could defend more easily and from which they could see far and wide. Also the land had been cleared by the Indians for corn growing and there was fresh water nearby. They decided on the latter site.

On December 12th they returned to the *Mayflower* with the good word that at last they had found a location for the settlement. Their home-coming was blighted, however, by the news that William Bradford's wife had been lost overboard in his absence. This death will be a mystery forever, as no mention is made of how or why she fell from the ship, although it is known she did accompany her husband.* There is no record of her body being found.

Her death must have been a heavy blow to her husband, although he makes no note of it except a single line in his history of the Plantation. Since suicide was considered a religious crime in those days it would be an unusual occurrence in the history of this God-fearing group.

On December 15th the *Mayflower* weighed anchor for Plymouth but had to put back because of storms. On December 16th the weather cleared and the ship left Cape Cod and eventually dropped anchor in Plymouth Harbor. The 17th was a Sunday, which was spent as usual in prayers, psalm singing and services.

On Monday, the 18th, a party went ashore with Master Jones and three or four sailors. They could not find any river deep enough at low tide to accommodate a sizeable boat but they were

* Women usually were not mentioned unless they died or gave birth to a child.

impressed with the site close to the harbor, the different kinds of trees, the grape vines, the herbs, and the wild flax and hemp. The records mention good clay available for pots but especially "many delicate springs of as good water as can be drunk." * The purity and potability of water must have been a surprise to a group brought up on beer because of the contamination of town and city water in England and Holland.

Two more exploring parties brought reports back to the *Mayflower* and much discussion ensued. It was finally decided that they should settle on the high ground near the harbor and start building a common house right away. Bad weather set in again, however, and the party on shore was cut off from the supplies on the ship because the sea ran so high the shallop could not return. In fact, the *Mayflower* itself was forced to "let fall our anchor and ride with three anchors ahead." **

* Mourt's *Relation,* ed. D. B. Heath, p. 41
** Ibid

Signatures of some of the Pilgrims—*Narrative and Critical History of America*

After the storm subsided, a few days before Christmas, the men worked hard cutting, sawing and splitting timber. In fact, they worked right through Christmas Day itself. The Pilgrims did not celebrate this occasion as it was not mentioned in the Bible and had become in England a rather ribald holiday with great feasting and drinking and general rowdiness. On the *Mayflower,* though, the master broke out some of the ship's beer for those who missed their usual merry England festivities.

On December 28th, a gun platform was hurriedly built on top of the hill that sloped to the sea, and in the afternoon, the grounds were measured out for 19 families. All men without wives were assigned to a family of their choosing in order that fewer houses would be necessary. The land was staked, so much to a person, according to the number of people in each family. Each parcel was about 8 by 50 feet so that a family of five would have the use of a lot measuring 40 by 50 feet. This was a small area but enough to start with, and certainly enough to defend against the Indians. They had not seen many but Indian fires were sighted by the lookouts almost every day.

On January 4th Myles Standish and a few men went to where a fire had been seen but found no one. On the way home they shot an "eagle." When cooked it tasted good "like mutton." Some fish were caught and clams dug but sickness, probably like our virus pneumonia but complicated with scurvy, set in and spread quickly among the weakened, exhausted company. Continued spells of foul weather contributed to the illness and hindered the building. However, Mourt's *Relation* states that by January 9th the common house, about 20 feet square, was almost finished except for thatching. Several family houses had also been started.

On February 17th an important meeting was held to establish military orders and Standish was formally chosen Captain. He was in a hurry to put up some kind of organized defense against the Indians and on February 21st they brought ashore three cannons (one weighed 1200 pounds!) and two bases. These they heaved up onto the gun platform.

OF THE ONE HUNDRED AND FOUR PASSENGERS
THESE DIED IN PLYMOUTH DURING THE FIRST YEAR

JOHN ALLERTON	THOMAS ENGLISH	ELLEN MORE AND	EDWARD TILLEY AND
MARY, FIRST WIFE OF	MOSES FLETCHER	A BROTHER (CHILDREN)	ANN HIS WIFE
ISAAC ALLERTON	EDWARD FULLER AND	WILLIAM MULLINS,	JOHN TILLEY AND
RICHARD BRITTERIDGE	HIS WIFE	ALICE HIS WIFE AND	HIS WIFE
ROBERT CARTER	JOHN GOODMAN	JOSEPH THEIR SON	THOMAS TINKER
JOHN CARVER AND	WILLIAM HOLBECK	SOLOMON PROWER	HIS WIFE AND SON
KATHARINE HIS WIFE	JOHN HOOKE	JOHN RIGDALE AND	JOHN TURNER
JAMES CHILTON'S WIFE	JOHN LANGMORE	ALICE HIS WIFE	AND TWO SONS
RICHARD CLARKE	EDMUND MARGESON	THOMAS ROGERS	WILLIAM WHITE
JOHN CRAKSTON SR.	CHRISTOPHER MARTIN	ROSE FIRST WIFE OF	ROGER WILDER
SARAH, FIRST WIFE OF	AND HIS WIFE	MYLES STANDISH	ELIZABETH, FIRST WIFE OF

Memorial to the Pilgrims who died during the first year of the colony
—*Plymouth Area Chamber of Commerce*

Myles * Standish must have rested easier but his peace was
short-lived as he and William Brewster were soon completely involved in nursing the sick. William Bradford had already been
stricken as had most of the other leaders like Carver, Winslow
and White. All work stopped for only six or seven people were
on their feet. Two or three died every day and, according to tradi-
tion, were quickly buried at night on Cole's Hill ** back of the
fort so the Indians would not know how much their number had
been diminished. The sick were taken ashore as soon as the disease
hit them, supposedly to keep them from contaminating the well
people, but the crew soon caught the germ and half of them
died. A small note on Master Jones' unpretentious kindness tells
how on February 9th he went ashore and shot five geese, had them
cooked and passed them out to the sick.

* There is some discussion whether this name is Miles or Myles but his signature
on display at the Pilgrim Hall in Plymouth clearly shows that he spelled it *Myles*,
at least in this instance. See also page 45.
** So named but much later.

47

It must have been a dreadful time. During this first year several families were totally wiped out (ironically the only one untouched was the Billingtons), 13 of the 18 wives died, 19 of the 29 single men and half of the crew. The children fared better: all seven girls survived as did ten out of the 13 boys. Certainly those who survived: "Strangers and saintly brethren from Leyden were now bound by common suffering, common courage, into a unique solidarity."*

Captain Standish wisely decided that emergency measures were necessary and every able man was allotted guard duty. This led on March 7th to the first case of discipline. John Billington refused to stand his watch and was sentenced to have his neck and heels tied together. (Bradford soon commuted his sentence but Billington continued to be a bad actor. In fact, he was the first murderer in the colony and in 1630 was hanged for it.)

On March 16th, one of several meetings was held to decide on military procedure and protection. Previous meetings had been interrupted by the sight of Indians, but this day, to everyone's amazement, a brave walked right into the meeting. He was tall, muscular and well-built, a fact discernible to all as he was almost stark naked. To top off the surprise of his sudden and casual appearance, he thus addressed the assembled company: "Welcome, Englishmen!"

Undoubtedly he received a somewhat reserved response but was given at his request some food and brandy. (He first asked for beer but the Pilgrims' supply had been exhausted.) He also was given some clothing—not requested—of which he would wear only an immodest assortment. He explained that he had come down the coast with one English captain by the name of Dermier who had been sent out by the Council of New England but had not returned to London. From him and other English seamen he had picked up his English and a liking for English food and liquor. His name was Samoset.

In a friendly manner he explained that the Patuxet tribe who usually inhabited that area had been wiped out by the plague.

* Fleming, Thomas J., *One Small Candle,* p. 176

That accounted for the empty Indian houses, the corn fields and the graves they had found. He also told them of the Wampanoags further west, whose chief, Massasoit, wanted to meet them.

Samoset spent the night, carefully watched, and left the next morning only to return in a few days with five more Indians. They, too, were friendly, talked of "trucking" or trading in furs and corn, but were interested mainly in the English food and baubles Samoset had received.

On his next visit Samoset promised that he would bring back a brave who spoke better English than he did because he had been kidnapped by an English sea captain, one Captain Waymouth. After the ship had been hijacked by Spanish pirates, he had made his way from Spain to London. There he had stayed several months being exhibited, questioned and entertained before getting passage back home.

In this manner did the Pilgrims hear about Tisquantum or Squanto, as he is most commonly known. The next time Samoset came, March 22nd, he brought Squanto along and he was to prove their great friend and ally who helped them in many vital ways to cope with the wilderness he knew so well.

For one thing, he instructed the settlers in planting corn, explaining to them that it would amount to nothing if the seed were simply stuck in the ground without fertilizer. For this purpose, he showed them how to catch alewives or herring which were making their spring run up the brooks. (They still do.) In each hill of corn they were to put about as many herring as seed. Then, after two or three days, they must post guards to keep away the wolves that would come after the rotten fish. Probably many a Pilgrim youth got a good scare on his night watch as the shining eyes of the wolves converged around him.

Squanto also showed them how to tread eels out of the mud at low tide and the Pilgrims found them very toothsome when cooked. Other kinds of fishing he helped with as well as the snaring of wild animals such as rabbits and deer. In short, the Pilgrims' standard of living must have gone up soon after his arrival, possibly accounting for the rise in health of the survivors of that nightmare of a winter. Or perhaps the infection had simply run its course.

Certainly Squanto had a hand in bringing Massasoit, chief of the Wampanoag tribe, to the Pilgrim encampment on March 22nd, a day that should be encircled by anyone studying this unique band of people. On this day a treaty of peace was arranged between white men and Indians that lasted fifty years. Its success was based on mutual needs and weakness, but credit for this should be shared by others besides Squanto, especially by Carver, Bradford, Winslow, and Standish.* Obviously a student of human nature, Standish sensed from the beginning that the Indians must be impressed with the English or they would not be their allies. Hence from the moment he and his people set foot on New England soil, he took pains to show that they had armor and guns and the courage to use both. He also could see by the Indians' colorful facepaint and decorations that they liked a good show. Therefore, at every opportunity he would drill his pocket-sized "army" in as smart a formation as he could muster. He suspected, as did the other leaders, that their every move was watched by Indian outposts in the woods, so they marched even to Sunday services with muskets at the ready and drums and trumpets often sounded across the wilderness. Standish would order the muskets fired with their impressive roar and flame, and he and the other principal men put to good use the supply of gayly colored bracelets and earrings made of glass beads, along with inexpensive knives which they had brought with them. Word had come back via ship captains that the Indians were childlike in their love for gaudy trinkets and adornment.

Standish was also one of the master minds and organizers for the ceremonious reception that Massasoit and his braves received. For one thing, the leaders had decided the day before to take all those who had lived for so long on the *Mayflower* off the ship. To be sure, Master Jones was anxious to be gone, for

---

* Other authorities disagree about Standish. Willison, for one, considered him to be short-tempered, dictatorial and possibly the cause of much discontent among both Indians and white men.

the *Mayflower* was already four months late in departing, but this evacuation of the ship swelled the number of those in the colony, thereby making it more impressive to a visitor.

The meeting between Massasoit and Carver was replete with details that make good reading for young and old as they are both so human and so meaningful. For instance, there was the hesitation as to who was to go to meet the Indian "delegation" when it appeared in the distance. He might never return. Edward Winslow, a young man apparently not lacking in either courage or diplomacy, was chosen. He soon won over Massasoit and his

Statue of Massasoit—*Corinthia Morss*

brother, Quadequina (ka-de-keen-a), with his welcoming speech and presents, including a pair of knives for Massasoit. After speeches of thanks by the Indians there was a good deal of discussion as to whom the Pilgrims should leave as hostage while Massasoit and his braves attended the meeting. It was also problematical whether the Indians would be willing to leave their bows and arrows, tomahawks and other weapons behind when they visited the colony. This was resolved, and Massasoit with 20 braves proceeded across the brook and approached the conference "table." Winslow was left behind—in some jeopardy because the chief had made it plain he admired Winslow's gun and armor and wanted to truck for them. Winslow apparently talked him out of it, and must have watched with interest while Massasoit was greeted by Standish and Master Thomas Williamson, the first two Pilgrims to advance toward the oncoming savages, who were painted to the eyes for the occasion. The chief was told that great King James saluted him with love and peace, which seemed to please him, whereupon Governor Carver appeared, ushered in with drum and trumpet. He escorted the chief to a partly constructed house where a green rug and three or four cushions had been placed. Brandy was passed around and toasts were proposed, whereupon Massasoit took a great swallow "that made him sweat all the while after . . . ." * Apparently he recovered, however, and they quickly started eating. A discussion of the terms of the peace followed and Massasoit, after talking them over with his braves, seemed pleased and agreed to them all.

These terms in brief stated that the English and the Wampanoags were to live in peace and as allies. If a white man was harmed by an Indian, the offender was to be sent to the white people for punishment. If any tools or other items were stolen, they should be returned. If either party had unjust war declared against them, the other would help. Any visitor from either side was to come unarmed.

Massasoit was not entirely without guile in treating the white

* Mourt's *Relation,* ed. D. B. Heath, p. 56

invaders so kindly. He was worried about his warlike neighbors to the south: the Nausets on the Cape, the Narragansetts in Rhode Island, the Pequots in Connecticut; and the Massachusetts tribe to the north. To hold them at bay he wanted the help of the white men with their guns and cannon. And the Pilgrims, on their part, needed the Indians' help against these unfriendly tribes and depended on their know-how in obtaining fish or furs, and in growing good crops. Even so it is remarkable that Massasoit found the Pilgrim ideals of love, peace and friendship logical and attractive so quickly and held his people to their contract so long. As has been said in this account and in others, the Pilgrims seemed to move forward against all kinds of adversity by sheer determination and a faith in God, or, as they would have explained it—by the will of God. That they were fortunate in some circumstances cannot be denied.

For instance, their landing near the tip of Cape Cod was providential. They might well have been blown down the south side where the Narragansetts probably would have had their provisions and their scalps before the year was out. The land at Plymouth (or Patuxet) that they chose, while not the richest, had already been cleared before their arrival. The Patuxets who had lived on it, had been most conveniently (for the Pilgrims) wiped out by the bubonic plague or some similar disease. Only Squanto was spared because he was kidnapped and taken aboard just before the plague struck.

The Pilgrims were also fortunate that Master Jones kept his *Mayflower* off shore during that first winter. Although hardly ideal, it served as a shelter and while it seems a ridiculously small vessel to modern eyes, it must have loomed as an enormous craft to the Indians. It commanded their respect as did the aggressive and determined actions of the exploring and construction teams sent to land and build in weather even the Indians seldom exposed themselves to.

But perhaps their biggest piece of good luck was Squanto.*

* One scholar commented to the author that he might have been planted by the Council for New England, which will show how much variety of interpretation there is about the details of the Pilgrim story.

He and Master Jones were at opposite poles, culturally speaking, but they befriended the Pilgrims at a time when their friendship made the difference between life and death.

❀　❀　❀

Apparently spring came early in 1621. (It can be late and cold in New England.) Crops of corn, peas and barley were planted and the morale of the group was high enough so that when, on April 5th, the *Mayflower* hoisted anchor for the return trip to England, not one Pilgrim left on her. However, it must have been a dire moment, as her sails disappeared over the horizon, to realize that they were now absolutely alone. They must survive on their own.

One great loss they suffered almost immediately. On a warm day while working in the fields, Governor Carver was taken suddenly ill (probably by a heart attack) and died a few hours later. A meeting was called soon after to choose a new leader and in an act of great wisdom, they turned to William Bradford. He was then a young man, about 31, but a natural and vigorous leader. Much of the future success of the colony can be laid to his wise and courageous guidance. He was to serve the colony for the next 35 years in some capacity and to act as governor or assistant governor 30 times.

One of his first decisions was to do something about their all-too-frequent Indian visitors. Friendship was one thing but the Indians interpreted their new treaty to mean they could drop in with their squaws and children at any time and receive food and presents. And they expected this hospitality to last several days.

Needless to say, this was a drain on the Pilgrims' combined larder. They had been able to build four public houses and seven dwellings but their gardens had not begun to bear very much, and the men had been too busy with carpentry, sawing planks, cutting thatch, and finding wattle-and-daub for the fireplaces to do much hunting or fishing.

So Edward Winslow, the perennial diplomat, and Stephen Hopkins were sent on a trip to Sowams, Massasoit's village. They

A view of Plimoth Plantation—*Corinthia Morss*

were to find out where it was and how far away in case they needed help, and to speak about the hospitality problem.

On the way they met other tribes, who welcomed them. Apparently tales of the white man's friendship and firmness had been spread around and this image was not dimmed by Stephen Hopkins, who, when challenged, killed a crow at 80 yards with his musket. The Indians well knew how hard it was to hit a crow at any distance, much less kill him.

Once at Sowams, a distance of about 30 miles, they were welcomed by Massasoit with appropriate dignity. They gave him several gifts, including a red robe edged with lace that greatly pleased him. Once the preliminary formalities were over, Winslow boldly stated the cause of their journey—that frequent friendly Indian visits were exhausting their supplies. He thereupon produced a copper chain which he suggested Massasoit put around the neck of any official visitor so they would recognize him as such.

Massasoit agreed to this with apparent affability and the conference continued in a friendly manner all day long. By evening the two Pilgrim delegates were very hungry but Massasoit explained that he had just gotten back from a trip and had no supplies on hand. This situation was not unusual, even for a chief, because it was Indian custom to gorge when there was food and go without cheerfully when there was none.

There seemed nothing to do but go to bed, and Massasoit insisted the two men share his with him and his wife. Accounts have it that this was hardly a regal couch as it consisted of a few planks raised off the floor an inch or two and covered with two or three thin mats. Other occupants included a plentiful supply of lice and fleas but the crowning blow was the arrival in the middle of the night of two braves who came in and threw themselves down on top of all. Said Mourt's *Relation,* "We were worse weary of our lodging than of our journey." *

The next day, whole villages poured in to see this new curiosity—two white men—and entertainment was provided in the form of races and wrestling matches. By noon Winslow and Hopkins were almost starved but the good news arrived that two large bass had been caught and were being cooked for them. This turned out to be true but they had to serve more than 40 people so that when the two Pilgrims left the next day they were completely tired out and considerably thinner than on arrival.

A young Indian leader, Hobomok, was chosen to accompany them home and decided to stay with them for an indefinite period as Squanto had done. Like Squanto he turned out to be a great asset and friend, especially on future diplomatic missions such as one that confronted them soon after they reached home.

The Billingtons, father and sons, seem to have been a first-class problem to the Pilgrims from the moment the *Mayflower* sailed from Plymouth, England. Mention of them crops up every so often in the old accounts but never more dramatically than when young John Billington, aged 9 ** or thereabouts, went out

* P. 66
** Sources conflict as to his exact age.

56

on a hunting trip, wandered off and failed to return. Winslow and Hopkins had just come back from their Sowams trip, reporting that friendship had been consolidated with the Indians, so Bradford decided to ask for help from Massasoit in finding the missing boy. The Wampanoag chief immediately sent out runners to neighboring tribes and located young Billington down on the Cape, safe and sound with the Nauset tribe, no less.

Bradford elected to leave immediately with a few men in the shallop. Because of a storm they hove to at what is now Barnstable harbor; then went on to Eastham where they were welcomed by a friendly young chief, named Iyanough, who put on a lobster feast and entertainment. The dancing was interrupted by an old woman who appeared, cursing all white men, as her son had been kidnapped by a Captain Hunt * ten or so years before, and she was still distraught about it. Bradford calmed her down with presents and a speech that claimed he and his brethren were as upset by Captain Hunt's actions as were the Indians and did not condone them.

The next day Iyanough accompanied the Pilgrim party to the home of the Nausets. There they were met by Aspinet, the chief, and hundreds of Indians with young Billington in the middle, completely covered with glass beads and undoubtedly grinning from ear to ear. He was handed over by a party of 50 braves with bows and arrows at the ready whom Bradford pacified with a gift of two very fine English knives.

A semi-peaceful parley was broken up by Aspinet when he told Bradford that the Narragansetts were at war with Massasoit and had captured him. Bradford and his party immediately started for home, fearing that Plymouth itself might have been taken over also by the Narragansetts. Unfavorable wind delayed their return but they found Plymouth unharmed on their arrival. However, Squanto and Hobomok were dispatched to find out from

---

* Not to be confused with Captain Waymouth. Actually, Squanto met Captain Hunt after this Englishman had picked up a cargo of fish at Monhegan in what is now Maine. Supposedly Squanto led 20 or so Indians on board Hunt's ship to show them that his stories of the white men were true. Hunt feasted his visitors— Squanto had departed—then closed the hatches and sailed away to sell his cargo as slaves. (See A. Molloy, *Five Kidnapped Indians*, pp. 130-132.)

the neighboring tribes what was going on and meanwhile Bradford and Standish began earnest military drill for all able men—32!

On Hobomok's return, he told of arguments between the tribes and vengeance sworn against Squanto for befriending the white men and promoting the peace treaty. He had been captured by a chief named Corbitant, Hobomok said, and was probably now dead.

A short conference was held, after which Standish and ten men set out for Nemasket to rescue Squanto. They arrived at Corbitant's village about dusk and planned a bold move—to attack his house at midnight, an hour when all would be asleep. At the appointed time, they went charging in to the complete hysteria of the men, women and children inside. (Neither Squanto nor Corbitant was there.) Standish threatened the men with instant annihilation if they did not produce Squanto but he said the women and children would go free. (An interesting note states that after his speech many young men claimed to be girls in order to be spared!)

The house was easily taken over in spite of the number of braves outside. After the skirmish, Hobomok climbed on the roof and called Squanto, who appeared shortly after, unharmed! Standish continued his warnings to the tribe, now well aroused from their sleep but also well subdued by the events. He said that if Massasoit were not returned uninjured by the Narragansetts, the Pilgrims would make war on them. This was an amazing statement from the commander of a standing army of 32, but again Standish's firmness worked. In a few days the leaders of many tribes arrived, anxious to promise peace and share the treaty of mutual protection. And, to every one's satisfaction, Massasoit himself returned, unharmed.

The confrontation with Aspinet of the Nausets and Corbitant of the Wampanoags made Bradford, Standish and the other leaders decide to consolidate their position further. They had managed to make peace with their neighboring tribes of Indians but how about those further north—the Massachusetts tribe?

"Weymouth dugout," Braintree Historical Society, Braintree, Mass.—*Plimoth Plantation*

"Massasoit bowl," Peabody Museum, Salem, Mass.—*Plimoth Plantation*

Something must be done to prevent possible attacks and also more should be known about the land and people of that area.

Consequently on September 18 the shallop set out for Massachusetts Bay with ten colonists and Squanto to explore the region and trade with the Indians. The Pilgrim leaders had not forgotten that they had debts to pay off to the London company, the Adventurers, that had financed their expedition.

The journey north was full of tense situations as the tribes around what is now Boston Harbor were known to be warlike and undependable. However, when they landed at Squantum they found recently deserted villages and corn fields. Pressing on, they came to heaps of picked corn guarded by many squaws, the men of the tribe having fled. Thanks to their Indian interpreters, and the Pilgrims' "gentle carriage" the women were soon convinced of the visitors' peaceful intentions and set about preparing a good meal of boiled cod and other food. Soon an Indian man appeared, "shaking and trembling for fear." When calmed down and reassured, he promised some beaver skins to trade.

The next day the party crossed over to Charlestown and had an equally peaceful time of it, after which they marched to Nanepashemet's grave in Medford (he had been a famous chief of the Massachusetts tribe, leaving at his death his wife to rule in his place). Again some trading was accomplished and there were promises of more in the future.

One interesting incident is recounted of the beautiful beaver skins worn by the squaws as they worked in the corn fields. These women realized that the skins were valuable and insisted on taking them off and trading them. Since they had on nothing else, they pulled branches off the trees to cover their nakedness and managed in the eyes of the visitors to be "more modest than some of our English women are." *

The old accounts are full of such human interest notes. For instance, as the shallop sailed out of what is now the Boston-Quincy harbor, apparently the Englishmen marvelled at the site. Mourt's *Relation* states, "Better harbors for shipping cannot be

* Mourt's *Relation*, ed. D. B. Heath, p. 79.

every one settled in for the winter and shared what food and clothing there was.

In spite of this friendly meeting, early in 1622 apprehension about a possible Indian attack increased, and it was decided to build a stout stockade around the whole settlement. Within this each family had a house and a garden plot. In May, news of an Indian massacre in Virginia was received and the first muster of the militia was called. In June a fort was started.

The summer brought good crops but by November it was obvious with the influx of 50 to 60 men on the *Charity* and the *Swan* that more grain would be needed to get through the winter. Bradford took a party to the Massachusetts Indians and brought back some corn, but Squanto, who accompanied them, died while on this expedition.

Early in 1623 Weston arrived with a party of rough, coarse would-be settlers who at first were helped by the Pilgrims but whose unruly conduct soon ended this. All the colonists were delighted when they moved on to start a settlement at Wessagusset (now Weymouth). Soon, however, news arrived of their continued bad behavior—they stole corn from the Indians and annoyed their women.

In the meantime, a messenger came from Massasoit asking that Edward Winslow come to him as the chief was very sick. Winslow found him suffering from a bad case of constipation, which he cured. (This is a story in itself.) As a result, grateful Massasoit confided to him that the Massachusetts and the Nauset Indians were going to destroy Wessagusset and then go on to attack Plymouth.

Instead of waiting for this to happen, Bradford decided to send a small force with Standish in charge to Wessagusset to size up the situation. The captain found the Weston Colony practically at the mercy of the Indians. The settlers were treated like servants or worse, had nothing to eat but shellfish, and were constantly threatened and tormented. Standish himself was taunted, but bided his time until he could get some of the offending Indians into the house where his soldiers were temporarily lodged. When the door was securely barred, he pulled a knife out of an Indian's hand and stabbed him fatally. The rest of his "posse" then killed two more and hanged a fourth. Whereupon the Indians ran off, and the fight was over. Some of the Wessagusset men returned with Standish to Plymouth. The others sailed to Monhegan (Maine), thereby abandoning the ill-fated colony. An interesting detail of this tiny military engagement was that the head of one of the Indian dead was brought back to Plymouth and put on show there . . . a grisly but customary act in that era.

By April of 1623, hard times set in. Crops had been planted but, of course, had not matured. The winter's grain supply had been used up. The bounty of the sea kept the Pilgrims going but severe drought occurred in May, June and July and the corn crop wilted badly. Discontent grew, and it was decided to change the planting and cultivation procedure. From the beginning, the Pilgrims had labored for the community and the harvest was divided among all the families, regardless of who had done the most work. To ease the resultant grumbling and to give a needed incentive to individual men and families, each settler was granted a one-acre plot to plant and care for as his own. Bradford states, "This had very good success for it made all hands very industrious and . . . gave for better content. The women now went willingly to the fields . . . which would before allege weakness and inability." *

The drought continued, however, and was so bad that the Governor called a day of humiliation and many prayers. Soon after, rain did fall—enough to revive the corn plants and human spirits, too. "Behold another providence of God," said Bradford.

Even though their prayers about rain were answered, it was a long wait before the harvest and the arrival of corn mush and bread on their tables. Lobsters, clams and striped bass washed down by spring water remained their principal food although a kind of beer was concocted from pumpkins, parsnips and walnut tree chips.

* Bradford, William, *Of Plymouth Plantation,* ed. S. Morison, p. 120

Cultivating the soil to plant corn at the Plantation. Note the Fort Meeting-house in the background—*Plimoth Plantation*

In August, 1623, the *Anne* and the *Little James* arrived with about 60 people, including some of the Pilgrim congregation that had been left behind in Leyden. Like previous arrivals the Pilgrims' old friends were dismayed at the gaunt appearance of the colonists and their threadbare clothes. They were also surprised at the unrelieved fish diet, lacking as it did their customary meat, bread and beer.

Ten "Particulars" also came in those ships. These were the first of many men sent over by the London Adventurers to settle and work for themselves. They were a separate group under their own government and were not required to work for the good of all as the Pilgrims were. Yet they were given, by order of the Adventurers, the same amount of food and land as the "Old Comers" or Pilgrim passengers.

Naturally, this upset the original colonists, who had worked hard for what they had and were loath to share it. However, the Particulars were not admitted as citizens or Freemen and could not vote unless they agreed to work for the community and be-

Interior scene of Plimoth Plantation showing guns and furniture of the period—*Plimoth Plantation*

lieved in the Pilgrim ideals and faith. (Actually, those who remained in Plymouth were so admitted in 1627 but each Freeman had to apply for the privilege of joining and be voted in.)

Late in 1623 it was decided to allot them land and freedom to work for themselves but they had to pay a tax of a bushel of Indian wheat and could not share in Indian trade. This was reasonable since this trading was the only way the Pilgrims had of paying off their debt to the Adventurers.

One new arrival on the *Anne* was most welcome: Alice Southworth. She and her husband had been of the Leyden group but after his death she had elected to return to England. William Bradford, however, had conducted a successful courtship by mail, and persuaded her to share his life in the New World. Their wedding, which took place soon after her arrival, must have been quite a show. For one thing, Massassoit attended with four chiefs and 120 warriors. He wore a black wolf's skin over his shoulders and a black blanket around his waist. Undoubtedly the other Indians also sported their best furs and other adornments.

One can only wonder how the Indians reacted to the occasion. Unfortunately they left no written records.

The 1623 harvest was good and the fall and winter passed more comfortably than the year before. This winter (1623–1624) was the first one without famine.

Early in 1624, the level of subsistence was further improved by the return on the *Charity* of Edward Winslow, who had been sent over to get supplies and explain the situation to the Adventurers. He brought back clothing and other necessities and also some cattle—a bull and three heifers. These were most welcome and were the start of a cattle business that was to put many a Pilgrim family ahead economically in the vital years of the 1630's and 40's. As Samuel Eliot Morison says, "The Pilgrims' troubles were by no means over; but from now on it was not hunger or Indians that bothered them but human folly." *

* Morison, Samuel Eliot, *The Story of the "Old Colony" of New Plymouth*, p. 99.

In 1624 John Lyford, an Anglican minister from Ireland came over. He and his family were welcomed at first as much criticism had come from England because the colony, for all its purity of religious aims and practices, had never had a clergyman who could give communion and perform other official rites of the church. The reason had been that the Leydeners were waiting for their beloved pastor, John Robinson, to join them and fill that important role. (He died in 1625 without ever making this long-planned trip.)

Because of this the colony held back on recognizing Lyford as their official religious leader. Although he was given a house and food, he was not ordained by the Pilgrim church.

This was fortunate as Lyford soon proved to be a real troublemaker. Before long, it was discovered that he had been a bad actor at home and had left Ireland because he had trouble with women in his parish. As Mr. Morison puts it, he was a real "wolf" with the girls in his congregation.*

Lyford had not expected his past to catch up with him so quickly and was enraged at not being officially installed in Plymouth. He decided to make trouble for the Pilgrims in general and Bradford in particular and wrote highly critical letters home saying that the colony was mismanaged and that Bradford was a poor leader.

In some manner, Bradford heard about these letters and a most dramatic situation built up. Knowing that the ship, the *Charity,* taking the Lyford letters back to England was to sail the next day, Bradford and a few friends rowed out under cover of darkness and persuaded the master, William K. Pierce, to let him copy the letters, reseal them, and send them on. They turned out to be as derogatory and full of malicious lies as he expected, but he said nothing about them until a meeting of the Freemen or General Court was called.

Bradford's own explanation of this delay is nicely expressed: "The reason the Governor . . . concealed these things the longer was to let them ripen that they (Bradford and his supporters) might better discover their (Lyford and associates) interests and see who were their adherents." *

Lyford was brought before this body and accused of being a traitor. He denied the charge; whereupon Bradford produced his copies of the letters. Public opinion had risen to great heights against him and the evidence was too much. Lyford finally admitted his guilt and was banished from the colony.

The original letters arrived in England, however, and stirred up much resentment among the Adventurers, who were already disappointed in the return they had had on their investment.

John Oldham, one of Lyford's unsavory "adherents," had come over six months or so after Lyford, and had gone along with his efforts to undermine Bradford's rule of the colony. Oldham also was brought before the Freemen, and both were sentenced —Lyford was to leave Plymouth in six months and Oldham right away. Lyford eventually moved down the coast and spent the last years of his life as an Anglican minister in Virginia. Oldham reappeared unlawfully in Plymouth in 1625 and, as a punishment, was made to run the gauntlet of two lines of able Plymouth men equipped with muskets. They propelled him forcibly down the alley with the butt end of these, and, according to record, his language was awful. But he did get the point and moved to Nantasket (Hull) and then to Watertown where he lived an apparently honorable life until he was murdered by Indians in the Pequot war.

Other settlers of all kinds were beginning to arrive, not only in Plymouth but in the towns that were springing up along the northern Massachusetts and Maine coast such as Cushenoc (Augusta), Penobscot (Portsmouth), Winnesunnet (Chelsea) and Shawmut (Boston). Then there were the growing villages nearby—Nauset (Eastham), Commaquid (Barnstable), Sandwich, and Yarmouth to the east. (Of course, there was no Cape Cod Canal at that time so the land was unbroken to the tip of

* Bradford, W., *Of Plymouth Plantation,* ed. S. Morison, p. 150

the Cape.) Duxbury, Marshfield (first called Rexham) and Scituate lay to the west and Taunton and Rehoboth to the south. All of these from Shawmut south and east were included in the Plymouth colony as well as others now part of Rhode Island.

The settlement at Wessagusset continued to have a curious history. Shortly after Weston left, Captain Robert Gorges came from England to begin a plantation there, but left after a few months. Then sometime in 1624 a Captain Wollaston and his followers took over the Weston cabins and were joined by a London lawyer, one Thomas Morton. Wollaston found New England not to his taste and moved to Virginia, but Morton and a few carefree associates set up an establishment at Ma-re Mount in what is now Quincy. It soon was appropriately called Merry Mount (or Merrymount) as Morton offered liquor and guns to the Indians in return for furs. He seems to have been genuinely friendly with the Indians and tales of gay dances around a maypole with jovial squaws soon found their way to Plymouth.

Bradford and the other leaders did not condemn other ways of life and did not interfere if their neighbors behaved morally, but the traffic in firearms at Merrymount increased to the point where they could no longer overlook it. They did not want the Indians to get more power or to find some reason to cut down on their fur trade with Plymouth.

A raid was decided on and in June, 1628 Captain Standish led a small group of men to Merrymount where Morton's garrison had holed up in his house. They decided to rush the place —a brave act as they knew the group had guns—but the strategy worked. It turned out that the defenders were so "over-armed with drink" * that they could hardly hold up their guns, much less shoot them accurately. Standish knocked Morton's gun out of his hands with a sword and the rest surrendered.**

Morton was tried and sentenced to return to England but it took a number of men and a block and tackle to get him on board the ship before it sailed.

* Bradford, W., *Of Plymouth Plantation,* ed. S. Morison, p. 209
** It is amusing to note that Morton left an entirely different version of this in his *New England Canaan.* It has been discounted by historians.

Cultivating corn at Plimoth Plantation—*Plimoth Plantation*

In England, trouble increased for the town of Plymouth as more tales were sent over about their narrow religious views. Many of these were false but, as has been pointed out, it *was* true that newcomers were not allowed to join the Pilgrim congregation unless they were voted in as members. Other complaints mentioned in reports concerned the small land allotments, and the frequent presence of foxes, wolves and mosquitoes; but what the newcomers hated most was the hard work. The captain of the *Little James* said in a letter probably written in March 1624 that there were too many women and children and "do-nothings."

He wrote, "If it were not for some few who are both honest, wise and careful, . . . the plantation would fail and come to no thing." *

Perhaps even the slothful realized this situation because in 1624, although the Leydeners or "Old Comers" were now greatly outnumbered, Bradford was again elected Governor.** In that year John Smith relates that Plymouth's population was 160 and 32 houses had been built.

In 1625 some horses were imported. They were not exactly thoroughbreds but adequate for work. The cattle, pigs, sheep and goats had multiplied, and consequently the food in general had improved.

By 1627 Bradford must have felt the pressure of criticism and realized that the strife between the two factions of Newcomers and Old Comers over land holding and payment of debts must be settled if the colony were to remain a single unit.

Hence he and the other leaders arranged with the Adventurers in 1627 to divide the assets and the land between all the men, even those who were not members or children of members of the original company. A single man received one share of company properties; married men got one share for each member of the household over 16. Fifty-eight men shared in this manner and the settlers were divided into 12 companies, totalling 156 people. All acreage was surveyed and divided: each share to be 20 acres and a house, depending on the household, and given out by lottery so as to be fair. (In this way Bradford escaped the accusation of favoritism.) The livestock were also divided—one cow and two goats for every six persons. All meadowland, however, was to be held in common as it was scarce.

As for the debt to the Adventurers, Bradford was anxious to consolidate it rather than have so many responsible for it. Hence, he and seven associates—Brewster, Winslow, Alden, Allerton, Standish, Howland and Prence—called the "Under-

---

* James, S. V. Jr., ed. *Three Visitors to Early Plymouth,* pp. 36-37
** Bradford was elected 30 times between 1621 and his death in 1657. Edward Winslow and Thomas Prence also served several terms as governor.

takers," agreed to pay the full price of £1800 at the rate of £200 a year. In return this group would have a monopoly of the Indian trade for six years.

However, they spent much of their trading money to bring the remainder of the Leyden families to Plymouth. Also, when they sent shiploads of beaver and otter skins to London that should have more than paid off the debt, they were cheated out of most of the money by James Sherley, one of the Adventurers, and Isaac Allerton, one of the original *Mayflower* arrivals. At least, that is how some tell the story.

At this point, it is obvious that the colonists were poor businessmen—naive, trusting and totally unused to figuring out compound interest and other commercial details. They came to

One of the goats at the Plantation has fun on a hurdle (portable fencing used to pen in animals)—*Plimoth Plantation*

realize that they were being "had" but did not know how to cope with the situation. A good account of their financial dealings may be found in *Debts Hopeful and Desperate* by Ruth McIntyre.

Perhaps their attention business-wise was turned elsewhere to more profitable ventures. They had established fur-trading posts in Maine, Connecticut, and on the Buzzards Bay side of the Cape. These did well for some years although there were instances of cheating there too, especially in Maine, plus attacks by the French.

Still fur money did pay off some of the debt, and there was surplus corn for trading, but most of the new prosperity came from raising cattle. By 1628 the Pilgrims discovered they could dispose of cows and pigs at a good profit to their neighbors, the members of the Massachusetts Bay Colony, who had started to arrive in large numbers. These were Puritans who fled from the persecution of Charles I, just as the Pilgrims had been forced to leave England because of their disagreement with James I. These colonists were different from the Pilgrims, especially in one respect—they were wealthy. Even though they had spent large sums on ships and supplies, they needed farm animals on arrival and could afford to buy them from the Pilgrims. More than 2000 new people had arrived by 1630 so the market was good. Since the allocation of land in 1627 in the Old Colony (a name commonly used from now on), farms outside Plymouth had sprung up in Duxbury, Marshfield and Kingston, and much of their acreage was devoted to cattle raising.

The exodus to these towns eventually drained Plymouth of a good percentage of its original settlers. The population actually decreased between 1630 and 1644 and problems arose because many of the Freemen or voters found it inconvenient to go back to Plymouth on Sunday for church services as required, or to attend the General Court. For instance, by 1637 Brewster, Standish, Alden and Prence had moved to Duxbury, and Edward Winslow to his stepson's house in Marshfield.

As for church services, the First Parish Church (now Unitarian) had been formed in Scrooby, England, in 1607 and

John Alden House, Duxbury—*Corinthia Morss*

brought to Plymouth in 1620. It is the oldest church organization in New England. By the time the Massachusetts Bay Colony came into being the Plymouth church had ceased to be Separatist, and helped the new colony start its own Congregational Church. The First Church in Duxbury was formed in 1637 and other towns followed suit.

This solved the long-walk-to-church problem for the inhabitants of outlying towns but the Freemen were not eased of their required attendance in the General Court until 1638 when it was decided that towns could elect representatives instead of sending all their Freemen to each meeting. In fact, there had been a clarification of government structure in 1636 when the Governor and Assistants along with four men from Plymouth, two from Scituate and two from Duxbury drew up a sort of constitution for the colony called the *General Fundamentals*. This laid down many excellent laws, the first one stating that no law could be made without the consent of the Freemen or their representatives. There was to be an election every year of the Governor and Assistants by the Freemen. Every man was to receive equal justice, no matter what his financial or social position was. No one could be punished except by law. Any offender could have a trial by jury and could object to the individual jurors if he wished. Anyone 21 years old or more could dispose of his property as he desired. Congregational churches were to be protected and the livelihood of the minister taken care of by their individual towns.

This extraordinary document, which was so politically sound and ahead of its time, defined the rights and obligations of the Freemen, but they had other worries. One was the wide scope of Bradford's and the Old Comers' rights under the so-called Warwick Patent granted in January 1630. (The original patent of 1621 had no land boundaries and was useless by this time.) The 1630 patent *did* give definite boundaries to the Old Colony land from the Cohasset River to Narragansett Bay, including all Cape Cod and both sides of Buzzards Bay; also it enlarged the grant on the Kennebec River in Maine. All this territory and the right to govern it were given to William Bradford, his heirs and his associates forever.

Bradford considered the term "associates" to mean the Old Comers but even so it looked like government by the well-to-do few to the majority of the colonists. Public opinion rose against it but there was no need to take action because Bradford and the Old Comers soon realized the situation and signed over their governing rights under the patent to the General Court of Freemen in 1641. It was a generous and gracious action. They also gave up title to all unassigned land. For this the General Court voted £300 to the 58 Old Comers as well as three big tracts of land.

The boundaries in the Warwick Patent started arguments with the Massachusetts Bay Colony, which by now was larger and more prosperous than Plymouth. These went on for 20 years before the present Old Colony Line between them was settled.

Meanwhile a depression had struck New England that was especially bad in Plymouth. In 1640 the Civil War in England ended the persecution of the Puritans, so they no longer had to move out of the country. Most of the Pilgrims' earnings had come from the sale of cattle to the Bay colonists and the price of a cow dropped 75 percent in the early 1640's. Many farmers left to go to more prosperous settlements.

There was by now more moving about generally. As has been said, towns had sprung up on the Cape and along the trails inland. Each of these had its own government and sent two deputies to the General Court. There was trading at the forts on Buzzards Bay with the Indians, at Windsor on the Connecticut River with the Dutch, and on the Kennebec with the Indians and the French. There was also trading at the town fairs that were

Mother sheep with lambs on the Plantation—*Plimoth Plantation*

beginning to be held on holidays or oftener in some places. Practically no money changed hands—the system was to swap what you had for what you needed. The Old Colony exchanged corn, cattle, sheep, horses, and so on for cloth, tools, utensils and other scarce (to them) objects.

Trade had grown up with the West Indies so the New Englanders could obtain sugar, molasses and spices in return for their salt fish, pickled beef, or lumber. Horses were also in demand down there. Not that many ships went direct from Plymouth —instead they sailed to the wholesale merchants in New Haven, Salem, Newport or New London, and bartered for their goods there.

There were more and more contacts like this with the other colonies and with different tribes of Indians. As the colonies expanded, there was rising tension with the red men, who could already see their lands dwindling as the foreign visitors formed new settlements.

In fact, the newer colonies were progressing in many ways more rapidly than Plymouth. For instance, Roger Williams had come to Plymouth toward the end of 1631, had met favor with the Old Comers and been invited to be their preacher. However, he soon disagreed with the Pilgrims on many subjects and went to Salem. Three years later he quarreled with the church leaders there and settled in Rhode Island. He obtained a royal charter for the Providence Plantation in 1644 and Connecticut secured one in 1662. (Plymouth never did obtain one.)

The Indian Wars were brewing and in 1637 the Pequots attacked the English in Connecticut. Winslow was sent down to assess the trouble, and in June the General Court agreed to give help.

Because of this unrest, in 1642 further fortification of Fort Hill in the Plantation was ordered. In 1643 a watch-house was built and a town watch instituted. This was the year when Plymouth joined the New England Confederation, a coalition of representatives from Massachusetts Bay, Connecticut and New Haven (then a separate colony), formed for mutual protection against the Indians. They met in the capitals of the colonies and voted on the number of troops and the amount of money each would provide, according to the population. For instance, in 1645 Plymouth's population was around 2,500 and its soldier quota was 40, the same as Connecticut and New Haven. Massachusetts Bay had to provide 190, which gives an idea of how swiftly that colony had grown.

Before describing King Philip's War, which was more of a conflict, considering the population, than most history books relate, it might be interesting to look at general life in the Old Colony in this 1630–1660 era.

To begin with, the colonists had by this time gotten a good view of the variety of New England weather. Besides the usual heat, drought or prolonged rain in the summer, and the dampness, chill and frequent snowstorms of the winter, they were shocked by a full-scale hurricane in 1635, apparently as bad as the New England one of 1938. Bradford says,

> "The 14th and 15th of August was such a mighty storm of wind and rain as none living in these parts, either English or Indian ever saw. . . . It came with violence in the beginning to the amazement of many. It blew down sundry houses and uncovered others. Divers vessels were lost . . . it caused the sea to swell above 20 feet right up and down (ed.—a good description of abnormal tides) and made many Indians to climb into trees for their safety." *

There were several floods and an earthquake in 1638, and another in 1658. All in all, it is a wonder that there are *any* 17th century houses left in Plymouth County.

Another evidence of typical New England weather even in those early days is the presence in Plymouth of a 17th century English ship called the *Sparrowhawk*. Bound for Virginia, she made the trans-Atlantic trip in good shape with 25 passengers but was wrecked on a Cape Cod sandbar. All aboard were saved and spent the winter of 1627–28 in Plymouth, parcelled out

* Bradford, William, *Of Plymouth Plantation,* ed. S. Morison, p. 279

among the families, but the vessel was sanded over by repeated storms and remained that way for 200 years. Finally, a similar storm but blowing the other way, uncovered the hull, which was salvaged, reassembled, and can now be viewed at the Pilgrim Hall. It is the only genuine remnant (the hull is more or less complete) of a 17th century vessel, used to bring English settlers to this country. After viewing its small size—only 45 feet over-all!—it seems remarkable to most people that as many colonists arrived as did.

The health of the colony after that first terrible winter of 1621 was good. However, a smallpox epidemic hit them in 1633, killing among others, surgeon Samuel Fuller.

The practice of medicine was still primitive, although by the middle of the century several physicians had come over from London. General education also was slight. When a boy could do his sums, write his name and read a page in the Bible, he was usually through his learning. Not until 1677 was each town required to have a school.

Harvard College was founded in 1636 and opened in 1638 but more Puritans than Pilgrims attended it. Thomas Prence, who was Governor of the Old Colony in 1673, was a student there along with Josiah Winslow, son of Edward, and Isaac Allerton, Jr., but few others. Not many Pilgrim sons had any higher education.

The lack of transportation as well as money was probably a factor. There were few roads anywhere, only paths. Travellers rode horses or went by sea. Practically all merchandise was shipped by boat. The Pilgrims, however, did not take naturally to the sea. Also Plymouth harbor would allow only small trading and fishing vessels, so most of the families stayed on their farms, at least as long as the Old Comers were alive.

In reality, the Pilgrims were not especially interested in free enterprise. The Biblical life as described in the New Testament was their goal and they took care that no one amassed a fortune by sharp trading. Up to the middle of the 17th century they regu-

The cooper was a busy man at the Old Colony. He made barrels and tubs of all kinds.—*Corinthia Morss*

lated prices and wages and fined any man if he overcharged or made an exorbitant profit. Community efforts persisted in most towns, as can be seen by their cutting wood together for the winter, then allotting it to each house-owner. Alewives were netted after their spring run by appointed individuals and divided among the farmers as needed for fertilizer.

There were a growing number of craftsmen: carpenters, blacksmiths, mill workers, weavers, tanners, coopers. And in Taunton, where iron ore was discovered, a furnace was started where tools, nails, kettles, chains and other necessary items were manufactured. This became a prosperous town as did Scituate, where shipbuilding flourished. The lumber for hulls and masts, the hemp for rope, and the flax for sails were produced locally, and the necessary iron bolts and braces came from Taunton.

These two towns had well-to-do craftsmen and merchants but the farmers all over Plymouth Colony were comfortably off,

Cooking a meal Pilgrim style at the Plantation—*Plimoth Plantation*

too. There was no money but little actual poverty either. Not too many newcomers moved in because of the strictness of the laws. No one could buy land or settle anywhere without permission, nor could they leave either. Also little privacy was to be had— for instance, a man could not build a house in the woods for his family. He had to stay in the confines of the town where church attendance was required and taxes had to be paid. Offenders were brought before the General Court or assembly of Freemen.

The Governor and his Assistants formed the supreme judicial court. Wrongdoers of small crimes were fined and locked up in the stocks for a while or publicly whipped. They were rarely jailed because that was costly. In fact, there *was* no jail in the colony for 20 years. Drunkenness cost five shillings plus an hour in the stocks. The charge was double the second time and triple the third. Other crimes were dealt with in a similar fashion and original sources show that the whole array of sins of the flesh and other wrong doings were coped with.*

However, justice, mostly based on the Bible, seemed to prevail in these early townships. It was simple, logical, and apparently effective. Torture—to obtain a confession or evidence—was not allowed. A man could not be forced to bear witness against himself, nor was any one burned at the stake or mutilated. Even the Quakers who made trouble in Sandwich in 1656 were only whipped and sent on their way. They received harsher treatment elsewhere as did "witches" or women with supposed supernatural powers. A few were brought to trial in Plymouth but none was hanged or burned as in Salem and Boston. Children did not have a bad time of it, mostly because they were made to feel part of the family almost as soon as they could walk. They had small chores such as feeding the chickens and the pigs, helping with household chores, and weeding. They also had small pleasures like playing ball and fishing in the summer, and skating and sliding in the winter. And, oh bliss, there was little or no school.

However, no activities took place on the Sabbath. From twilight on Saturday until twilight on Sunday, no one did anything but the necessary chores and meal preparation. There was a long church service in the morning and another in the afternoon.

With this determined attention to the spiritual man, it is no wonder that efforts were made to christianize the Indians. Some of these were successful; others were not.

From the first the Pilgrims were friendly with the Indians because they needed their help and support, and they insisted on "buying" their land, not just taking it. However, they paid nothing for the Plymouth area because there were no living Patuxets to buy it from. Squanto could have sold it to them but the

* Bradford, W., *Of Plymouth Plantation,* ed. S. Morison, Appendix X. *Opinions of Three Ministers.* Answers of Rev. John Rayner, pp. 404-413

thought apparently did not occur to anyone. In fact, the idea of selling land was a new one to the Indians. They accepted tools, clothing, cloth, and other commodities for tracts of land but then expected to keep living on it. The Pilgrims were tolerant of this attitude but an Indian neighbor had built-in inconveniences. By Pilgrim standards he was dirty, lazy and apt to take anything he could find, especially tools, poultry or pigs.

And the Indians, like most primitive people, were hard to change. The Pilgrims could not spare men for missionaries nor did they have any extra preachers, but efforts were made to convert the "heathen" in the early 1600's. Richard Bourne and Thomas Tupper in Sandwich tried to convert the Nausets in the 1640's and the Rev. John Eliot, known as "Apostle Eliot," preached to them in their language in 1648 near Yarmouth. The entire Bible was translated into the Algonkian language, and by 1670 there was a Indian Congregational Church in Mashpee. Other groups of "Praying Indians" were formed and preached to in their own language by English ministers like John Cotton of Plymouth, and it is estimated that by 1685 there were 1,439 Christian Indians in the Old Colony.* These remained loyal to the colonists through King Philip's War.

Philip, the chief of the Wampanoag Indians, was the son of the Pilgrims' old friend, Massasoit. He was a man of unusual ability and had been on good terms with the colonists until he felt their increasing numbers meant the destruction of the Indians. War did not actually break out until 1675 but, as has been noted, Plymouth had joined the New England Confederation in 1643 and had kept up military training during this time.

All healthy males between the ages of 16 and 60, except for ministers and schoolmasters, were part of the colony's militia and drilled regularly. Each one had to have a musket, a sword and ammunition. Those who could not afford a gun carried a pike (a long wooden shaft with a metal tip). The younger men were trained in Indian warfare while the older soldiers stayed home to defend the villages. In each of these a "garrison" house was des-

* Morison, S. E., *The Story of the "Old Colony" of New Plymouth*, p. 244

ignated that had loopholes in the walls through which flintlocks could be fired. It also had a stock of food and ammunition. At warning of an Indian attack, the women and children crowded into these garrison houses, a maneuver that saved many a settlement.

In January 1674 Sassamon, an Indian chief who was a convert to Christianity, was murdered on the way to warn Edward Winslow, then Governor of Plymouth, that King Philip was preparing for war. A contingent of white men went after the culprits, two Indians, and, according to some reports, hanged them. This was the match that lit the flame of war and nullified all the attempts at diplomacy over the last few years made by the Old Colony toward Philip. The following March, Indian raiding parties ranged over much of Massachusetts, Rhode Island and Connecticut, burning houses and ambushing hastily formed

View of the top deck of the Fort Meetinghouse—*Corinthia Morss*

militia. Although Philip had less than 500 warriors while Plymouth colony numbered over 5000 in population, the white settlements were widely scattered and very vulnerable to surprise raids. Philip's strategy was to attack one town at a time while his supporters to the north kept Massachusetts Bay so busy they could not send help. The little town of Rehoboth was the first to be sacked and burned, and Plymouth suffered about twelve casualties in a massacre at Eel River.

There is not room here to describe this war in detail but it is estimated that more than 1200 white men were killed and untold numbers of women and children. This was a high percentage of total manpower—a heavy blow to the colony as was the widespread devastation of houses, crops and livestock.

The atrocities committed by the Indians infuriated the colonists, many of whom retaliated in kind. Some of the Indian prisoners were shipped off and sold as slaves in the West Indies, and when Philip was killed, his body was quartered and left to rot where it lay. His head was displayed on a stake in the fort at Plymouth.

The war left Plymouth in a great economic depression which was not helped by an increase in royal taxes. Charles II died in 1685 and was succeeded by James II, who was pro-Catholic. The new governor of the Old Colony, Thomas Hinckley, tried to get a royal charter for Plymouth but did not succeed. Plymouth had always been a loyal and obedient crown colony but had not applied for a charter in the early days because they thought a royal governor might go with it. Then when their identity was at stake —Massachusetts and Connecticut both having received a charter —they were too late.

In 1686 Sir Edmond Andros was appointed Governor of the Dominion of New England (a combination of all the English colonies there) and became very unpopular because of the high taxes he proposed. In fact, in 1690 there was a tax revolt in Plymouth itself, one of the Old Colony towns that nearly went bankrupt during his administration. The General Court sent £100 to

Grave of Myles Standish, Duxbury—*Corinthia Morss*

Gravestone of Myles Standish, Duxbury—*Corinthia Morss*

London in March 1691 in another attempt to win a charter, but the money arrived too late to accomplish anything. Later that year Plymouth was forced to become part of the Massachusetts Bay Colony.

At this date Plymouth or the Old Colony ceased to be a separate entity and it is generally considered the end of the Pilgrim story. Certainly it is the end of the period that the museum, Plimoth Plantation, will cover. However, in the opinion of many, the real termination of the story came with the death of William Bradford in 1657 at the age of 67. Edward Winslow had died in 1655, not having returned from a trip to Jamaica sent by Oliver Cromwell. And the staunch Myles Standish departed this life in 1656. John Alden, who had moved to Duxbury, was the last to go of the Old Comers. He died on September 12, 1687, probably in his 86th year. (The exact date of his birth is not known.)

These were great men, especially Bradford, who ranks in accomplishments, leadership and vision with anyone in United States history. The men of the Pilgrim second generation in many cases were also unusually strong and talented but the old ideals, both religious and civic, had changed. The Plantation, a small group of people imbued with a unique purpose and the strength of mind and body to carry it through to accomplishment, was no more.

3

Plymouth—20th Century

THE history of modern Plymouth is similar to most towns of its size in New England. Many of the descendants of the Pilgrims moved to the Middle West or to larger cities although there is still a scattering of the old names in the Plantation area and along the coast, especially on Cape Cod in towns like Eastham. After the Civil War some small shipping continued as evidenced by town maps of the late 1800's showing the historic harbor crowded with wharfs. These were used by coal and grain and other small businesses, but the big industry was the Plymouth Cordage Company, makers of rope and fibre products. By the 20th century this had grown to be a huge enterprise with national and international sales. There were also two large knitting mills, the Mabbett Worsted Company and the Puritan Worsted Company.

The rope-making and knitting processes required many unskilled workers, and large numbers of Italian and Portuguese came across the ocean to get away from the poverty and lack of opportunity in their own countries. Once they had saved enough money, they brought over their wives and families, and settled down. This is why for almost half a century, parts of Plymouth were like foreign towns.

Across the United States industries like the Cordage kept the economic level high enough so these workers were able to exist

Major John Bradford House, Kingston—*Corinthia Morss*

fairly comfortably even on small wages. In Plymouth most of them lived in the two-family dwellings built by the Cordage for its employees. These spread gradually over the northern part of Plymouth while most of the old homes and public buildings of the colonial period were torn down to make way for them. The original Plantation had long since disappeared.

In 1920, for the 300th anniversary of the landing of the Pilgrims, town and state roused themselves to brighten up Plymouth. The commercial wharves were taken down and land at the harborside was built up and contoured to form a state reservation about Plymouth Rock.

A few fine colonial homes have been kept or restored in and around the site of the first settlement. They did not belong to the Pilgrims per se but are worth seeing. The only home of a Pilgrim father now intact is John Alden's in nearby Duxbury. (See p. 75.)

That of Major John Bradford (William's son) remains standing in Kingston. Both are charming, center-chimneyed dwellings, open to the public for a small fee. The site of Myles Standish's house in Duxbury may also be viewed as well as his grave there. (See p. 87.) The Society of Mayflower Descendants has its national headquarters in a beautiful 18th century mansion. The Sparrow House (1640), the Jabez Howland House (1667), the Harlow House (1677) which is said to contain the beams from the Fort Meetinghouse, and the Spooner House (1749) are varied examples of early American architecture.

Plymouth Area Chamber of Commerce

Mayflower Society House

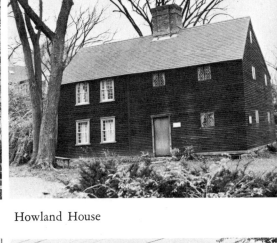

Howland House

Harlow House

Sparrow House

The first real efforts to preserve the heritage of the Pilgrims were made in 1769 when the Old Colony Club was formed. "Forefathers' Day" was first celebrated that year. Part of the celebration of 1774 was an attempt to move Plymouth Rock to the center of the town, but the boulder broke into two pieces. So only one half was moved, the remaining portion becoming enclosed in a wharf which was built around it. In 1880 the two parts were united and a marble monument erected over them. At the time of the Tercentenary Celebration, this early monument was replaced by the present portico given by the National Society of Colonial Dames and dedicated on November 21, 1921.

Whether the Pilgrims actually landed on the Rock in 1620 is not certain but some evidence indicates it was used by them, possibly as the basis of a small landing stage. An interesting booklet on the subject by Rose T. Briggs, published by the Pilgrim Society, ends thus: "It is the fact that they (the Pilgrims) landed and remained that matters, not where they landed. Yet it is no bad thing for a nation to be founded on a rock."

The Pilgrim Society was organized in 1820 to perpetuate the memory of the Pilgrims and their contribution to the American heritage. Pilgrim Hall was built by the Society in 1824, and houses a collection of Pilgrim artifacts and historical material. The Society was responsible for the erection of the Forefathers' granite monument, a huge pedestal surmounted by a female figure representing Faith set on a hill overlooking the town. The Society maintains the monument and grounds as well as Cole's Hill, site of the original graveyard of the early settlement and several historic markers. It has also been instrumental in obtaining other civic improvements and restorations.

After World War II, plans were announced for the creation of Plimoth Plantation, an outdoor museum to tell the story of the Pilgrim settlers. In two decades this project has attained national stature. Its development will be described in the next chapter.

In 1949 the "Plymouth Compact" was signed by civic leaders

Plymouth Rock (showing split)—*Corinthia Morss*

Portico over the Rock given by the National Society of Colonial Dames
—*Plymouth Area Chamber of Commerce*

Forefathers' Monument "Faith" given by the Pilgrim Society— *Plymouth Area Chamber of Commerce.*

and prominent business men to promote the possibilities of the whole area. An Industrial Development Commission was formed and an analysis of resources made. In 1958 the Plymouth Redevelopment Authority applied for permission for the Plymouth Rock area to be declared a National Monument. This was done in 1963.

Civic leaders now realize that besides the international attraction of Plimoth Plantation with its village, the *Mayflower II,* the Rock and the waterfront houses, they should count among their assets the beauty of the surrounding countryside and the charm of the neighboring towns. Kingston and Duxbury have been more fortunate than Plymouth in preserving their architectural landmarks and have street upon street of beautiful, authentic colonial homes.

The Plantation itself has contributed quite a lot to the economy of the town. Restaurants and motels flourish. Tourist business is seasonal but constantly rising. Eventually the museum may stay open all year, in which case a crowd visiting the Plantation in January would really find out what the Pilgrims had to put up with. As it is, if you go there in late fall, the wood fires burning in the big fireplaces of the Pilgrim houses feel comforting and smell good. They take you back in a most pleasurable way to the 1620's.

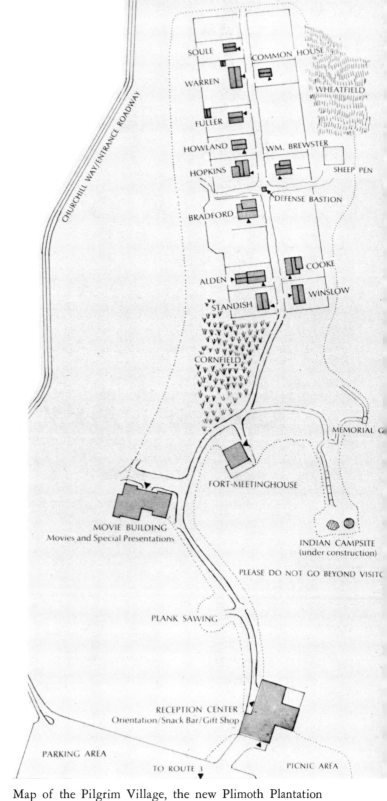

Map of the Pilgrim Village, the new Plimoth Plantation
Plimoth Plantation

4

The New Plimoth Plantation

Its Start and the Mayflower II

IN 1945, Ralph Hornblower, a summer resident in Plymouth, told the Pilgrim Society that he and his family had what they considered to be a worthwhile project. They wanted to recreate the original Pilgrim village approximately as it was in the first years before outside land was distributed and the Plantation ceased to be a small, compact unit. A substantial founding gift was offered and thus "The Pilgrim Village Committee of the Pilgrim Society" was started.

On October 2, 1947 Plimoth Plantation was incorporated as an independent institution with its purpose stated in the Articles of Incorporation as follows:

> ". . . the creation, construction and maintenance of a Pilgrim Village as a memorial to the Pilgrim Fathers; the management and operation of the same and the restoration or reproduction of antiquarian houses, buildings, tools and facilities; the historical education of the public with respect to the struggles of the early settlers, the expansion of that settlement and the influence of the Pilgrim Fathers throughout the world. . . ."

Ralph Hornblower's son, Henry, an archaeologist and anthropologist, became president and has enthusiastically served in this office since that date. After the incorporation, part of the founding gift was spent acquiring land near the present Plymouth golf course but most of this was taken by eminent domain for the Cape Cod Highway, now Route 3, not leaving enough for the village as planned.

The situation did not look encouraging but it was decided to test public reaction to the project by building the First House on the waterfront land cleared for the Tercentenary celebration. This was to be a typical Pilgrim dwelling, resembling the primitive houses first put up by the group after their landing. It was designed by Charles T. Strictland, an architect noted for his restoration of the Old North Church in Boston.

Completed in 1949, the First House was soon an obvious success as a visitor attraction and educational project, so plans were made to add more buildings to the waterfront exhibit and to construct a replica of the *Mayflower*. An experienced naval architect whose hobby was early sailing ships, William A. Baker of Hingham, was commissioned to design *Mayflower II*.

In 1953 the Fort Meetinghouse was built, followed in 1955 by the 1627 House, a slightly more sophisticated dwelling than the First House.

The First House and the 1627 House—*Corinthia Morss*

View of the Hattie Hornblower Estate where the new Plantation has been built—*Plimoth Plantation*

As this unit of buildings was stimulating public interest, a large gift of land was made to the Plantation by the Hornblower family. It was a bequest by Mrs. Hattie Hornblower, mother of Ralph Hornblower, of 50 acres near the mouth of Eel River on Plymouth Bay, three miles from Plymouth center.

This was a turning point in the fortunes and plans of the Plantation because the land was similar in topography to the original village site and would obviously make a fine place for a full-scale recreation of it. Also, there were outbuildings that could serve for temporary offices and exhibit areas. To top it off, the view was magnificent,—the same as from the original Plantation —across beautiful Plymouth Bay to the limitless expanse of the Atlantic Ocean.

In the meantime in 1954 Mr. Baker's plans for *Mayflower II* had been published and caught the attention of an English group interested in constructing such a vessel and finding it an appropriate home across the ocean as a symbol of British-American friendship. After all, the Pilgrims had come over in this ship and had lived in it five months or so while the houses in the Plantation were being built. It was a definite and essential part of the whole Pilgrim story. The London progenitors of what became *Project Mayflower,* Messrs. Warwick Charlton and John Lowe, reached an agreement with Plantation officials to build *Mayflower II* from Mr. Baker's plans, sail it across the Atlantic and present it to the Plantation. Their efforts were encouraged by the enthusiastic support of a wealthy fellow Londoner, Mr. Felix Fenston.

After several years of wide-ranging study, Mr. Baker had concluded that the 180-ton *Mayflower*, described only briefly in the journals of the Pilgrims, was a typical square-rigged trading barque. As Alan Villiers, the famous sea-captain who sailed her across the Atlantic, says in his book, *The New Mayflower*, "She was just some wandering little sailer that the Pilgrim Fathers could hire cheap, and nobody paid any attention to her then. We know she must have been old because one of her main timbers broke while she was in a storm. . . . She was only about 180 tons, which is less than the size of many tugs." *

For the building of the ship, *Projcet Mayflower* engaged Stuart Upham, a shipbuilder in Devon, England, whose ancestors had been constructing wooden ships for 200 years. Since it had been decided to have every detail authentic and hence necessarily handmade, this was a wise choice as some of the old craftsmen were still working in the Upham yard and could provide the needed skills.

The keel was laid July 4, 1955, and the story of the vessel's construction is a fascinating one. Anyone interested should read Alan Villiers' account and also that of the builder, Stuart A. Upham.**

* Villiers, Alan, *The New Mayflower,* p. 3
** Upham, Stuart A., *The Illustrated Story of How the Mayflower II Was Built.*

For instance, the working drawings were laid out in full size on a mould loft floor. Mr. Upham explains that this was a huge unbroken expanse of floor painted black, on which the plans of the ship were marked in chalk. Old tools were dusted off and sharpened for use by the "chippies" or shipwrights. The Devon countryside was searched for oaks that had limbs meeting in a crotch suitable for the "knees" of the vessel.

Once the ribs were ready, search was made for aged wood for the "tree-nails"—the wooden pegs that would hold the beams together. Success came with the finding of some ancient cider vats, over 120 years old, still in good shape and necessarily well-seasoned.

Caulking or filling up the seams between the planks of the ship was done with mallet and caulking iron. The oakum used came from the hemp of old mail bags and rope teased back to its original strands.

The rigging presented a problem as no one knew exactly what it had been like. Museums were searched, old models, documents and even 17th-century seals and coins were studied. The ropes were made by craftsmen at the Gourock Ropeworks in Scotland and the sails were woven of flax, a plant so ancient it is mentioned in the Bible. It has a very long fibre, finer than human hair, and makes a strong, long-wearing cloth. The sails were all sewn by hand.

Since the *Mayflower* was a 3-masted square-rigger, a bark, its rigging was complex but is well described in the Upham book, as are other details of outfitting and construction that will delight modern sailors.

Alan Villiers, who volunteered to be the captain for the trans-Atlantic voyage of the new-old ship, had picked his crew from experienced English seamen and yachtsmen, 33 in number. There were brief sailing trials after the ship came out of dry-dock, April 1, 1957. Finally ship and crew were towed from the Upham yard in Brixham to Dartmouth and then she was sailed to Plymouth, England, as the original *Mayflower* had been. She handled nicely.

On April 20th, the moment for departure arrived and the *Mayflower II* put out from Plymouth on the final voyage. As Villiers says, "At first it was calm and the ship was quiet and graceful in the sea. But when the sea became rough, how she could roll! Even some of the old sailors were seasick for a few days. But they continued to do their work." *

The voyage was uneventful except for the growing wonder of the crew as to how approximately 120 people could have existed on the ship when they felt so crowded with only 33. The weather tested their seamanship very little until, after seven weeks at sea, they neared Nantucket. Then the wind began to increase till it reached gale force and every sail had to be furled. As the saying goes, the ship was hove to. With bare masts they had to wait out the storm. This is the real test of a ship and *Mayflower II* gave a fine performance. She turned out to be not only a fitting memorial to the Pilgrims from their friends in England but also a well-constructed, safe vessel.

The day after the gale was clear and sunny and the ship stopped at Provincetown as had the first *Mayflower*. Then she sailed across Cape Cod Bay to Plymouth, Massachusetts, where a tremendous welcome awaited ship, crew and captain. There she was joined by a replica of the shallop, which had been built in this country.

The *Mayflower II* spent that summer (1957) in New York on display with trips during that first winter to Miami and Washington. Since 1958 she has been based in Plymouth except for the winter months. Literally hundreds of thousands of men, women and children have walked her decks and marvelled at the dangers and discomforts of that 1620 trip on such a small vessel. Kept in beautiful repair and with intelligent guides aboard to explain the craft and her history, she is indeed worth a trip to see.

* Villiers, Alan, *The New Mayflower,* p. 16

Mayflower II tied up at the State Pier, Plymouth—*Corinthia Morss*

Its Growth and Attainments

With the arrival of the *Mayflower II* in 1957, which was widely covered by television, radio and the press, public interest in Plimoth Plantation soared.

At the Eel River site there was nothing but the various buildings of the Hornblower estate until the Fort Meetinghouse was moved to its present location late in the year. Lots for the proposed village were marked out according to the original lay-out found in Bradford's history,* and the foundation of the Howland house was laid. The Howland Society, an organization of John Howland's descendants, had raised money for its construction and for its maintenance. It was completed in 1958.

1959 was the first full season for the museum, even though the only exhibit area was the sun porch of the old Hornblower House and the entrance was just a small booth at a sand lot designated for parking. At last they were in business.

During the next few years, more houses were added to the village complex as funds were raised. Their completion dates are given below. Nineteen houses in all are planned.

John Howland	1958	Myles Standish	1965
William Brewster	1959	George Soule	1966
Richard Warren	1959	Francis Cooke	1966
William Bradford	1959	John Alden	1966
Samuel Fuller	1960	Stephen Hopkins	1969
Edward Winslow	1961		

The order of construction was more or less determined by the money raised by the descendants for this purpose. In many cases these people had long ago formed their organizations, such as the Alden Kindred. This group now boasts thousands of members, all of them supposedly direct descendants of John. That is highly possible, since he and his wife, Priscilla, had 11 children, who inturn increased the population generously.

* This lay-out shows only one side of the street and halfway down the other. The placement of the other houses has been based on a study of available information and reasonable conjecture, says the Director, Mr. David Freeman.

The new Plimoth Plantation—*Corinthia Morss*

Any visitor will see that the houses are necessarily similar in architecture and design but vary in details. One of them, while looking the same, will be constructed in a different way.

As a result of a need to teach boys the use of hand tools and show them the crafts of long ago, a group of students from the Nashoba Valley Technical High School of Westford, Massachusetts, will erect the Francis Eaton house on the Plantation. Eaton was the only·carpenter among the Pilgrims and hence it is surmised that his house would have been fairly well built.

Plimoth Plantation will provide all materials for the Eaton recreation along with building plans, the services of its architect, its research facilities and the lodging of the students who erect the house. This is one of many projects originated by the Education Department of the Plantation to bring history closer to boys and girls by involving them in the Pilgrim era.

During this decade of house building, existing structures on the former Hornblower estate were adapted and readapted to the supportive, non-historical needs of the growing Plantation.

In 1964 a new Reception Center was constructed to house the vital functions of visitor orientation and food and sales services. The earlier buildings continue to serve for offices, research quarters, library, film and exhibit presentations, a photo laboratory and archaeological and other workshops.

Since 1964, time has been taken to reassess and review the accomplishments of the first twenty years and make plans for the future, always keeping in mind the founder's original purpose—to foster modern understanding of the Pilgrims and their struggle to create a new life in a new world. As a major tool in this respect, efforts are bent constantly to increase the lived-in aspect of the Pilgrim Village.

Presentation of the daily routines of the Pilgrims seeks to reach all of the visitors' senses. One can smell the food cooking, hear the Pilgrim hymns sung in the Meetinghouse, handle the house furnishings and examine the contents of storage chests and boxes.

In 1969, live animals—sheep, goats, and poultry—were added to the Village and the array of sensory effects. In fact, lambs have been born, and eggs are frequently laid by the hens, sometimes in full view of an admiring public. These creatures have presented some unexpected problems such as the sheep and goats eating up the garden, but have been such a success that a complete 17th-century farm with cattle and horses is on the planning board.

The contents of the houses have been carefully checked to make sure they include only the kinds of furniture, dishes and other objects used in the early 17th century and mentioned in the earliest household inventories. The cataloging of these estate inventories is a story in itself and shows how greatly the exhibits, research and education departments have grown and have learned to work together to present an authentic, well-rounded picture of Pilgrim life.

A Plimoth Plantation goat
—*Corinthia Morss*

A Pilgrim cupboard (repro-
duction)—*Corinthia Morss*

Interior of a Pilgrim home, showing type of bed used during the period
—*Plimoth Plantation*

The Plantation at Work

The Department of Educational Presentations

This department is in charge of presenting and explaining the exhibits to the public. Its jurisdiction covers the people who interpret them orally: the guides and hostesses. Naturally, its operation is closely integrated with the research, technology and crafts departments.

The guides and hostesses in the village houses and other buildings are carefully selected and trained. They wear authentic Pilgrim costume and are prepared to describe what life was like at that time and to answer questions about any phase of it. Some of them cook, tend the chickens and sheep, hoe in the gardens and saw wood. There is even a thatcher at work on the roofs of the new houses or patching up the old. He is an Irishman and proud of his work, claiming that thatch—which at the Plantation consists of long reeds or cattails carefully and thickly laid—if properly put on, will last seventy years, and is no more of a fire hazard than wooden shakes or shingles. However, the Pilgrim thatched roofs were eventually banned because sparks from the improperly constructed chimneys ignited them.

Instead of merely presenting a series of objects for people to look at and then go home and forget, the emphasis at the Plantation is on introducing visitors to some of the larger concepts that were basic to the Pilgrim way of life. For instance, the many aspects of Pilgrim economy—their struggle for existence, their trading with the Indians to pay off their debts, their relationship with the London Adventurers—are shown in different ways. The Fort Meetinghouse is a center for demonstrating the deep significance to them of religion. Seeing the group of lifelike mannequins listening intently to their preacher and hearing the old Pilgrim hymns sung with gusto (a professional recording) is a moving experience for visitors. The insecurity of the colonists' lives is driven home by the sight of the palisade, the gun mounts, and the heavy construction of the Fort Meetinghouse. A young visitor

A representation of a church service at the Fort Meetinghouse—*Corinthia Morss*

can learn from activities such as the survival crafts of wood-sawing, gardening and animal husbandry that the tiny group had to work very hard to stay alive. They had to stand and share together or they would have been absorbed by the wilderness or killed by Indians.

Supportive exhibits cover the Pilgrim background in England, Indian life as it was when the first settlers arrived, and other aspects of the times.

Thousands of school groups visit the Plantation during the season and background material is offered to the teachers beforehand so the classes can prepare for what they are to see. The exhibits in the Reception Center start them with an understanding of the world the Pilgrims left. An orientation movie follows. All of this makes the tour through the village and Indian encampment meaningful and lasting in effect.

Small groups of children have actually spent the night in the village houses. They prepared their food in the Pilgrim way, and found out first-hand what Pilgrim life was like. Two families have also done this and found it an informative experience, turning up homely facts of daily existence that no one bothered to record in the 1620's.

The Department of Technology and Crafts

In 1956 Mr. Henry Hornblower, president of the Plantation, made a fortuitous vacation trip to the Virgin Islands where he met an Englishman who was then Director of the St. Croix Museum. Cyril Marshall, trained in Birmingham as an artist and sculptor as well as a technician in metal work and wood craftsmanship, responded to Mr. Hornblower's enthusiastic description of the future Plantation and agreed to divide his time between Plymouth in the summer and St. Croix in the winter. This arrangement lasted for several years until he was persuaded to work full time at the Plantation.

To help interpret the Pilgrim story, it was decided to add mannequins to certain exhibits.* Mr. Marshall, with his technical training and ability in painting and sculpture, proved expert at turning out these figures. His success was based on a thorough study of each character before going to work. He scanned the early sources for any clue to appearance, habits and attitudes with the result that the figures became very lifelike.

The first mannequins used were department store castoffs. Made of papier mâché with plaster coating for faces, they were embellished by Mr. Marshall with personal features, wigs of human hair and appropriate clothing. Details for this project came from studying paintings and prints of the period, especially those done in Holland. The Dutch portrayed the common man more frequently than the English artists, who were apt to paint nobles or rich merchants who could afford to pay them for their labors.

The cloth used in the costumes—in fact, throughout the Museum was a study in itself, furthered considerably by research done at the Courtauld Institute of Art in London. This institute, founded and endowed by a wealthy cotton manufacturer, has made a specialty of studying fabrics from the earliest known tapestries, needlework and clothing to the present. It was discovered

* Used only on the *Mayflower* and Fort Meetinghouse as of 1970.

110

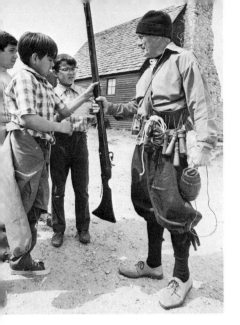

A guide explains the loading and firing of a matchlock musket used for demonstrations in the Village. These are Passamaquoddy Indian boys. *Right:* Pilgrim men cutting planks with a frame saw—*Plimoth Plantation*

through them and the Pilgrim inventories, for instance, that in the 17th century the farmers and others of the working class such as the Pilgrims wore quite colorful clothes instead of the staid black or grey in which they have been portrayed so long. Also, they undoubtedly wore loose-fitting garments instead of the tight bodices and sleeves of the traditional Pilgrim dress.

Mr. Marshall's mannequins were indeed works of art before he finished them. The red faces of some show exposure to New England weather; one small boy has a runny nose. All have human-looking complexions, made by "scumling," a process an artist may use on an oil painting. It modifies the final effect by overlaying a thin application of opaque color.

As for crafts, as pointed out, the visitor can observe the guides and hostesses carrying out the survival tasks of cooking, animal husbandry, wood-sawing, cooking and gardening. And, to show the importance of fire-arms to the colonists, a guide occasionally fires an ancient but well-preserved musket to the admiration of young visitors.

111

The Research Department

In 1967, the building of a full-time staff of trained research specialists, previously limited to one person, took impetus under Dr. James J. F. Dietz, anthropologist and assistant director. This team has made possible the expansion of modern scientific work on all facets of the Pilgrim story and its presentation.

The aim of the department is to communicate its findings to the public in general and the Plantation visitors in particular. The effort is well under way but will constantly be enlarged as research broadens the basis of knowledge and interpretation.

The exhibit program includes the two houses and the *Mayflower II* at the State Reservation and Pier, and the Village at Eel River. The newest project is a complete palisade around the Village, as close a re-creation of the original one as can be. A scale drawing has been based on descriptions in original sources and a careful comparison with other early American fortified villages.

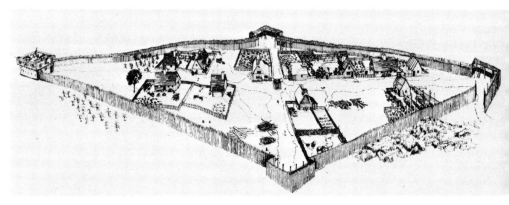

Scale drawing of the palisade—*Plimoth Plantation*

An Indian summer camp designed to simulate the daily living pattern of the aborigines of the Plymouth area has been developed on the actual site of just such a pre-Pilgrim encampment.

There is a film program that includes the daily showing of a color movie recreating the journey of the Pilgrims to the New World and their struggle for survival after they arrived.

For special showings, a film on thatching features the thatcher brought over from Ireland.

Another film, *Colonial 6,* produced by the Research Department, pictures an archaeological dig at the site of the home of Major John Bradford, son of the famous Pilgrim. This film is now standard fare at colleges and universities for students in archaeological and anthropological departments.

Actually, these students as well as those working for graduate degrees, find the Research Department and its well-organized files * of source material and artifacts a wonderful facility. And they will become even more useful as this department builds up its knowledge storehouse of the archaeology and ethnology of early American civilization, both white and Indian, going back to prehistoric days. It will also offer a place for analyses of American demography and all its vital statistics, considered dry and uninspiring for centuries but now a rich field in which to explore new concepts and do new things.

* These will be described later.

Bradford site in Kingston during the early stages of excavation in the summer of 1966—*Plimoth Plantation*

Artifacts found at Wellfleet site, 1969—*Plimoth Plantation*

Graduate students (many from nearby Brown University in Providence, R.I.) come to work at the Research Department in the summer. Some spend their time in the library or files, working up special subjects for scientific monographs. Others participate in the archaeological digs, three of which took place in the summer of 1969: the Titicut site in Bridgewater, Mass., a prehistoric Indian site, and an early 18th-century trading post on Great Island in Wellfleet Harbor, possibly the location of a residence, tavern and whaling station. To support this theory, remnants of cooking utensils, pipes, knives, a spoon and an English coin have been found along with a huge whale's vertebra that had obviously been used as a chopping block!

All such artifacts are cataloged, counted and recorded on punch cards in the research files at the Plantation.

Plimoth Plantation has five different kinds of these files: a Pictorial or Graphic File; a Primary Source File; an Indian File; an Architectural File, and an Estate Inventory File.

This is the way they work. Take a painting by Jan Steen, a Dutch painter who lived in the Pilgrim era, 1626–1679. A card from the *Pictorial File* with this painting on it might show 1) costume, 2) ceramics, 3) furniture, 4) cooking utensils, 5) eating utensils, 6) food, 7) fireplace construction, 8) window or other architectural details, 9) domestic animals, 10) child rearing, 11) family life, 12) household activities, 13) hair styles, 14) tools, 15) weapons, and many other details. There would be a punched hole on the edge of the card for each of these categories, so that when a stylus is put through a particular hole, all cards with information on that subject stay on the stylus; all others drop down.

The same system holds for the *Primary Source File*. On similar cards are glued Xeroxed copies of original source material relating to the Pilgrim period between 1500 and 1700. For example, Mourt's *Relation*, Winslow's narrative, Bradford's history and many 17th century letters have all been indexed into 88 categories, two pages per card with the volume and page reference on each one.

There is a similar file on Indians. This indexes the written material of the early 17th century, furnishing any ethnographic material on Indian groups living in the Plimoth Plantation area when the Pilgrims arrived. There are several hundred of these cards and they contain virtually all the available early accounts of Indian activities and appearance.

The *Architectural File* contains data on houses, shops, churches, barns, stockades, inns, etc. of the Pilgrim era as provided by books, prints, paintings, photographs, and artifacts.

The *Inventory Index File* contains type-script copies of wills and death inventories found in the Registry of Deeds at Plymouth from July 1, 1633 on. In this year it became law, just as in England, that when a man died, his will and a complete inventory and valuation of his possessions had to be filed with the civil authorities.

These inventories, while simply lists of *things*, are revealing and supplement the scanty information available on the Pilgrim households. They tell the value, color, material, number and location of most of the tools, furnishings, clothing, weapons and countless other items the Pilgrims lived with. All these reflect the Pilgrim way of life and are illuminating to anyone studying the period. Naturally, they are especially valuable to the exhibits department in furnishing the Village houses.

Still another unique kind of file houses the *Archaeological Collection.* This consists of all artifacts from each site or dig grouped into related subjects. They are all dated, correlated and classified, and include such categories as: animal bone (wild and domestic), ceramics, iron objects, glass, nails, clay pipes, eating utensils (they did not have forks!) and so on. Each of these is tagged as to identity, probable age, where found, etc., and placed in a drawer of a certain color. For instance, anyone interested in spoons or coins would only have to look on the color chart and pull out the drawer painted with the designated color.

Analysis of artifacts goes on all the time—first, to determine in which classification each belongs; second, to study its part in the Pilgrim civilization. For instance, in the excavation of the Great Island Site, scores of broken pipe stems were found. The bore of each one of these is measured because it has been learned that the older the pipes the larger the bore was. In this way it may be possible to learn such facts as approximately when and how long this island settlement existed and to have hypotheses confirmed by the finding of spoons and coins of a certain era in English history in the same dig. Also, comparison of these artifacts with others in the area may yield valuable information.

Fragments of pottery (called "shards" by archaeologists) are analyzed as to color, hardness and temper. Clay has to have a binder to hold it together and the Pilgrims apparently used gravel and grits. Many of their bowls were brought from England and are medieval looking; the later 17th-century ones were decorated. Locally produced ware was red in color and apt to be plain.

As far as food is concerned, work on the bones found in refuse piles shows that the Pilgrims ate mostly beef supplemented by sheep, goats, and poultry. Surprisingly enough, few wild turkey or wild animal bones have been found, indicating that after the settlement became well-established the Pilgrims relied on domestic animals and fish, undoubtedly varied with quantities of clams, oysters and lobster.

All of this research adds new dimensions to the cultural ecology of the period. In fact, the research program concentrates more on the study and interpretation of the Pilgrim culture and background than on the historical events that took place in their time. The latter have been so thoroughly researched for so long that uncovering new information will be a rare event. However, intelligent, painstaking modern research such as is done at the Plantation has already filled some knowledge gaps in the life of those days and changed old concepts such as those concerning the actual construction of the Pilgrim houses.

The first recreated houses were built with stone chimneys and hearths because stones had been found in the early excavations of foundations and they are so plentiful in New England. However, as more foundations were uncovered, it was obvious there were not enough stones for such large chimneys. This discovery jibed with the recent dismantling of authentic 17th century houses in the southwest of England, which revealed that the chimneys were made of wattle (brush) and daub (clay), not stone. The Pilgrims lived in such cottages in England and would naturally have built similar ones here, especially as such construction would take less time than stone masonry, and they were confronted from the start with a pressing need for living quarters and protection from the elements.

Another example of the emphasis on presenting only what is known to be true is the stitching on the sheets and pillow cases on the beds in the houses. It is an exact copy of old stitching found in existing remnants of 17th century bedding, and painstakingly worked by female members of the Research Department.

Still another instance of devotion to authentic detail can be found *in* the cloth bags hanging by some of the Plantation fireplaces. While they might easily have been stuffed with plastic, shaped in the right forms, they contain real hams. These are occasionally sliced as part of the food cooked daily in the houses.

The Research Department is indeed trying to eliminate the guesswork and supposition once draped around the Pilgrim image. They are determined to present life at Plimoth Plantation as closely as possible to what it really was.

The Membership Department

Plimoth Plantation, like many other museums, encourages men, women and families to join its "family" and become members. *Individual* membership is $10 a year. *Family* membership is $25 yearly and allows all members of a family to visit the Plantation free of charge. *Executive* membership ($35) permits unlimited admission to exhibits for the member and a guest accompanying him and 10 special admission cards. *Corporate* membership costs $100 and includes 50 passes a year to the Plantation.

The department keeps a close relationship with all members through The Plimoth Plantation Newsletter, issued frequently. This describes developments at the museum, changes in personnel, and in other ways keeps the membership up to date. All members are urged to attend the Annual Meeting in May to take guided tours and hear reports from the department heads. It is a delightful occasion, much enjoyed by both staff and membership.

The Public Relations Department

This department has grown rapidly along with Plimoth Plantation itself and the public interest in it. Its duty is to keep up this interest and inform the news media of any new developments, accomplishments or acquisitions.

To do this 10 to 12 releases are sent out a year and there are usually at least two good photographic releases for use in Sunday supplements. In addition many requests are received for articles in newspapers and magazines. The people on these assignments are given every help possible as well as the use of the Plantation library. The script must be sent in first and its purpose and point of view approved.

The use of the Plantation name in radio or TV commercials is not encouraged but photographs and transparencies are provided on demand for text books. Specific educational TV programs and photographic studies are filmed there but previous arrangements must be made so that visitors are not disturbed in any way.

*   *

Most Americans think of the Pilgrims at Thanksgiving time. However, those who have actually been to the Plantation are apt to have more recurrent thoughts.

The *historians* revel in the careful documentation of men, events and dates. *Scientists* applaud the archaeological and anthropological achievements and the store of material. They approve the possibilities for research and writings, and the discussion seminars and shop talks. *Economists* delve with enthusiasm into the well-cataloged information on the Pilgrims' business deals, their trading and land contracts, and their many financial probthought and argument in the Pilgrim methods of keeping law lems. *Students of government and civic affairs* find rich fields for

119

and order, yet accommodating their ways to the needs and challenges of both their Indian neighbors and the English new-comers. *Theologians* have long pored over the evidence of the Pilgrims' great faith in God and their attitudes toward those of other beliefs. Such rich ground is here for the trained mind, interested in any one of these facets of Pilgrim thought.

However, in the opinion of the author the Plantation's greatest gift to America probably is its presentation of the Pil-grims as *people.* To visit the Plantation and see its ways of life is to shake hands, to talk, to sit around with these early Ameri-cans. To feel the biting chill off the water is to know one of their physical hardships, to eat the cornbread prepared on the hearth of a little house in front of a roaring fire is to sample one of their pleasures, to see the little lambs come running when they are called to supper is to feel the homely reality of their life.

The Plantation makes *people* of the Pilgrims, not just shadowy figures in history.

Bibliography

NOTE: Many of the following books are out of print and are labelled O.P. However, some of them may be found on public library shelves or in their rare book rooms. Where information is incomplete, it was not available. J. indicates juvenile titles.

Baker, William A. *The New Mayflower.* Barre: Barre Press, 1958

Banks, C. E. *The Planters of the Commonwealth.* Baltimore: Genealogical Pub. Co., 1967

Bradford, William. *Of Plymouth Plantation* 1620–1647, Samuel Eliot Morison, ed. New York: Knopf, 1952

————. Worthington Chauncey Ford, ed. Boston: Houghton 2 vols., 1912

————. Harvey Wish, ed. (paperback) New York: Capricorn Books

Briggs, Rose T. *Plymouth Rock.* (A pamphlet) Boston: Nimrod, 1968

Burrage, Henry S. *Early English and French Voyages, 1534–1608.* New York: Scribners, 1930

Campbell, Mildred. *The English Yeoman in the Tudor and Early Stuart Age.* London: Merlin, 1960

Dalgliesh, Alice. *The Thanksgiving Story.* New York: Scribners, 1954 (J)

Demos, John. *The Little Commonwealth.* New York: Oxford University Press, 1969

Dexter, Henry M. *The England and Holland of the Pilgrims.* Boston: Houghton, 1906 (O.P.)

Dunton, John. *Letters Written from New England 1686.* New York: B. Franklin Print Society #4, 1966.

Fleming, Thomas J. *One Small Candle.* New York: Norton, 1964

Foster, Genevieve. *The World of Captain John Smith.* New York: Scribners, 1959 (J)

Gleason, Archer. *With Axe and Musket at Plymouth.* New York: American Historical Society, 1936 (O.P.)

Hall, Elvajean. *Pilgrim Stories.* (A revision of the Margaret Pumphrey Stories.) Chicago: Rand McNally, 1964 (J)

Hall-Quest, Olga W. *How the Pilgrims Came to Plymouth.* New York: Dutton, 1946 (J)

James, Sydney V. ed. *Three Visitors to Early Plymouth.* Plymouth: Plimoth Plantation, 1963

Langdon, George D., Jr. *Pilgrim Colony, A History of New Plymouth 1620–1691.* New Haven: Yale University Press, 1966 (Also paperback)

Leach, Douglas E. *Flintlock and Tomahawk: New England in King Philip's War.* New York: Macmillan, 1958 (paperback) Norton, 1966

Luckhardt, Mildred Corell, ed. *Thanksgiving—Feast and Festival.* New York: Abingdon, 1966 (J)

Mather, Cotton. *Magnalia Christi Americana.* 2 vols. 1852, New York: Russell, 1967

McIntyre, Ruth A. *Debts Hopeful and Desperate.* Plymouth: Plimoth Plantation, 1963

Miller, Perry and Johnson, T. H. *The Puritans.* New York: American Book, 1938. (paperback) Anchor Books, Doubleday, 1956

Molloy, Anne. *Five Kidnapped Indians.* New York; Hastings, 1970 (J)

Moody, Robert E., ed. *The Mayflower Compact.* Boston: Old South Association Leaflet #225

Morison, Samuel Eliot. *The Story of the "Old Colony" of New Plymouth 1620–1692.* New York: Knopf, 1956 (J)

Morton, Nathaniel. *New England Memoriall.* Cambridge: 1669, Plymouth: Danforth, 1826

Morton, Thomas. *New England Canaan.* (Originally published 1883) New York: B. Franklin Print Society, 1967

Mourt's *Relation.* Heath, Dwight B., ed. *A Journal of the Pilgrims at Plymouth* (paperback) New York: Corinth Books, American Experience Series #19.

————. Boston: Massachusetts Historical Society, Vol. 8, Series 2, 1802 (O.P.)

Palfrey, John G. *History of New England.* Vols. II and III (5 vols. in all) Boston: Osgood, 1884; A.M.S. Pr.

Peterson, Harold L. *Forts in America.* New York: Scribners, 1964 (J)

Plymouth Church Records 1620–1859. 2 vols. Boston, 1920 (O.P.)

Plymouth Colony Records. D. Pulsifer, ed. Boston, 1861 (O.P.)

Plymouth Town Records 1636–1783. 3 vols. (O.P.)

Pory, John. *Lost Description of Plymouth Colony*. Champlain Burrage, ed. Boston, 1918 (O.P.)

Powers, Edwin. *Crime and Punishment in Early Massachusetts*. Boston: Beacon Press, 1966

Smith, Bradford. *Bradford of Plymouth*. Philadelphia: Lippincott, 1936 (O.P.)

Smith, E. Brooks and Meredith, Robert. *The Coming of the Pilgrims*. Boston: Little, Brown, 1964 (J)

———. *Pilgrim Courage*. Boston: Little, Brown, 1962 (J)

Stephens, John P. *Towappu, Puritan Renegade*. New York: Atheneum, 1966 (J)

Upham, Stuart A. *The Illustrated Story of How Mayflower II Was Built*. Plymouth: Plimoth Plantation, 1960

Vaughan, Alden T. *New England Frontier-Puritans and Indians, 1620–1675*. Boston: Little, Brown, 1965 (also paperback)

White, H. C., Wallenstein, R. C. and Quintana, R. *Seventeenth Century Verse and Prose*. Vol. 1. New York: Macmillan, 1951

Willison, G. F. *Pilgrim Reader*. New York: Doubleday, 1953 (O.P.)

———. *Saints and Strangers*. New York: Reynal & Hitchcock, 1945 (paperback) Ballentine

Winslow, Edward. *Good Newes from New England*. London: 1624; Ward, 1897 (O.P.)

Winsor, Justin, ed. *Narrative and Critical History of America*. 8 vols. Boston: Houghton, 1884 (O.P.)

Winthrop, John. *The History of New England*, James Savage, ed. Boston: Phelps & Farnham, 1825; Little, Brown, 1853 (O.P.)

Wright, Louis B. *The Elizabethans' America*. Cambridge: Harvard University Press, 1965

Ziner, Feenie. *The Pilgrims and Plymouth Colony*. New York: American Heritage, 1967 (J)

Index

125

Quadequina, 52

Raleigh, Walter, 20, 26
Rayner, Rev. John, 83
Reformation, 14, 15
Rehoboth, 70
Rigdale, John, and wife, 31
Robinson, John, 20, 25, 27, 68
Rogers, Thomas, and son, 31
Roman Catholic Church, 13, 14
Rutman, Darrett B., 12

"Saints," 28-29, 48
Samoset, 48-49
Samson, Henry, 31
Sassamon, 85
Scrooby, 16, 22, 23, 28, 74
Separatists, 16, 24, 27, 28
Shallop, 40-45, 57, 60
Sherley, James, 73
Sickness, The Great, 46-48
1627 House, 98, 99
Smith, Capt. John, 9, 18, 20, 26, 43
Society of Mayflower Descendants, 91
Soule, George, 31, 104
Southworth, Mrs. Alice, 67
Sowams, 54-55, 57
Sparrowhawk, The (ship), 79
Sparrow House, 91
Speedwell, The (ship), 27-28
Spooner House, 91
Squanto (Tisquantum), 49-50, 53, 57-58, 60, 63, 83
Standish, Capt. Myles, 28, 31, 39, 40, 42, 46, 47, 48, 50, 58, 63, 70, 72, 74, 87, 88, 104
Standish, Rose, 28, 31
State Reservation and Pier, 112
"Strangers," 28-29, 48
Strictland, Charles T., 98

Swan, The (ship), 63

Taunton, 70, 81
Thanksgiving feast, 61, 62
Tilley, Edward, and family, 31
Tilley, John, and family, 31
Tinker, Thomas, and family, 31
Trade, 60, 63, 73-74, 77, 78
Trevore, William, 31
Turner, John, and sons, 31

Upham, Stuart A., 100-101

Villiers, Alan, 100-102
Virginia, 26, 35, 63, 70

Warren, Richard, 31, 39, 104
Warwick Patent, 76
Waymouth, Capt., 49, 57
Wessagusset, 63-64, 70
Weston, Thomas, 26, 27, 63
Weymouth dugout, 59
White, William, and wife, 31; 39, 47
Wilder, Roger, 31
Williams, Roger, 78
Williamson, Thomas, 31, 52
Willison, George F., 12, 30, 50
Winslow, Edward, 11, 12, 31, 39, 47, 50, 51-52, 54, 57, 61, 63, 67, 72, 74, 88, 104, 115
Winslow, Elizabeth, 31
Winslow, Gilbert, 31
Winslow, John, 62
Winslow, Josiah, 80
Winslow, Kenelm, 62
Wish, Harvey, 10
Wollaston, Capt., 70

Yarmouth, 69, 84

Zwingle, Huldreich, 15

128

14668